PEOPLE
IN THE NEWS

Tom Cruise

Lucent Books, San Diego, CA

Titles in the People in the News series include:

Garth Brooks
Sandra Bullock
George W. Bush
Jim Carrey
Tom Cruise
Bill Gates
John Grisham
Jesse Jackson
Michael Jackson
Michael Jordan
Stephen King
George Lucas
Dominique Moceanu
Rosie O'Donnell
Colin Powell
Princess Diana
Christopher Reeve
The Rolling Stones
Steven Spielberg
R. L. Stine
Jesse Ventura
Oprah Winfrey
Tiger Woods

PEOPLE
IN THE NEWS

Tom Cruise

by Joanne Mattern

Lucent Books, San Diego, CA

Library of Congress Cataloging-in-Publication Data

Mattern, Joanne
  Tom Cruise / by Joanne Mattern.
    p. cm. — (People in the news)
Includes bibliographical references and index.
  ISBN 1-56006-827-2 (alk. paper)
  1. Cruise, Tom, 1962– —Juvenile literature. 2. Motion picture actors and actresses—United States—Biography—Juvenile literature. [1. Cruise, Tom, 1962– 2. Actors and actresses.] I. Title. II. People in the news (San Diego, Calif.)
  PN2287. C685 M38 2001
  791.43'028'092—dc21
                                                    00–010559

✓ YA/CRUISE, /T.

Table of Contents

Foreword   6

Introduction
A Hard Road to Success   8
Chapter 1
Growing Up—and Taking Charge   10
Chapter 2
Early Struggles and Successes   24
Chapter 3
Working with Giants   41
Chapter 4
Taking Control   57
Chapter 5
Family Life   72

Notes   83
**Important Dates in the Life of
  Tom Cruise**   87
For Further Reading   89
Works Consulted   90
Index   91
Picture Credits   95
About the Author   96

Foreword

FAME AND CELEBRITY are alluring. People are drawn to those who walk in fame's spotlight, whether they are known for great accomplishments or for notorious deeds. The lives of the famous pique public interest and attract attention, perhaps because their experiences seem in some ways so different from, yet in other ways so similar to, our own.

Newspapers, magazines, and television regularly capitalize on this fascination with celebrity by running profiles of famous people. For example, television programs such as *Entertainment Tonight* devote all of their programming to stories about entertainment and entertainers. Magazines such as *People* fill their pages with stories of the private lives of famous people. Even newspapers, newsmagazines, and television news frequently delve into the lives of well-known personalities. Despite the number of articles and programs, few provide more than a superficial glimpse at their subjects.

Lucent's People in the News series offers young readers a deeper look into the lives of today's newsmakers, the influences that have shaped them, and the impact they have had in their fields of endeavor and on other people's lives. The subjects of the series hail from many disciplines and walks of life. They include authors, musicians, athletes, political leaders, entertainers, entrepreneurs, and others who have made a mark on modern life and who, in many cases, will continue to do so for years to come.

These biographies are more than factual chronicles. Each book emphasizes the contributions, accomplishments, or deeds that have brought fame or notoriety to the individual and shows how that person has influenced modern life. Authors portray their subjects in a realistic, unsentimental light. For example, Bill Gates—the cofounder and chief executive officer of the software giant Microsoft—has been instrumental in making personal computers the most vital tool of the modern age. Few dispute his business savvy, his perseverance, or his technical expertise, yet critics say he is ruthless in his dealings with competitors and driven more by his desire to maintain Microsoft's dominance in the computer industry than by an interest in furthering technology.

In these books, young readers will encounter inspiring stories about real people who achieved success despite enormous obstacles. Oprah Winfrey—the most powerful, most watched, and wealthiest woman on television today—spent the first six years of her life in the care of her grandparents while her unwed mother sought work and a better life elsewhere. Her adolescence was colored by promiscuity, pregnancy at age fourteen, rape, and sexual abuse.

Each author documents and supports his or her work with an array of primary and secondary source quotations taken from diaries, letters, speeches, and interviews. All quotes are footnoted to show readers exactly how and where biographers derive their information and provide guidance for further research. The quotations enliven the text by giving readers eyewitness views of the life and accomplishments of each person covered in the People in the News series.

In addition, each book in the series includes photographs, annotated bibliographies, timelines, and comprehensive indexes. For both the casual reader and the student researcher, the People in the News series offers insight into the lives of today's newsmakers—people who shape the way we live, work, and play in the modern age.

A Hard Road to Success

F EW STARS BURN as brightly in Hollywood as Tom Cruise. Over the past twenty years, he has become one of the most popular actors in the world. He has starred in blockbuster movies, lives a jet-setting life, and is married to Nicole Kidman, another popular and attractive movie star.

Tom Cruise poses proudly with his star on the Hollywood Walk of Fame in 1986.

But Cruise's life was not always so charmed. As a child, he faced many traumas and difficulties. His family moved so many times that he attended fifteen different schools. After his parents' painful divorce, the family struggled to make ends meet. And a learning disability called *dyslexia* made Cruise the butt of jokes as he struggled with schoolwork.

There were many negative elements in Cruise's childhood. But without those difficulties, he might not be the star he is today. Every obstacle life threw in Cruise's way became a challenge to overcome. And Cruise overcame those challenges—a learning disability, difficult scripts, unsuccessful films, unwanted media attention—through determination and hard work. By taking control of his life, Cruise became a success, both professionally and personally.

Cruise is admired for the hard work that has brought him success in Hollywood. But he has even more respected for his personal life. The sad memories of his childhood made Cruise determined to become a good husband and father. Tom Cruise is a superstar, both on and off camera.

Chapter 1

Growing Up—and Taking Charge

FROM THE OUTSIDE, Tom Cruise appears to have the perfect life. He is one of today's most popular and respected actors and a genuine sex symbol for his many fans. His work in such films as *Jerry Maguire* and *Mission: Impossible* has made him one of the highest-paid stars in Hollywood. And his performances in *Rain Man, Born on the Fourth of July,* and *Magnolia* have won him the admiration and respect of some of the industry's leading directors and his fellow actors. Cruise's personal life is also successful. He has been married to actress Nicole Kidman since 1990 and is the father of two children.

But Cruise's life has not always been perfect. His childhood was filled with upsets. His family moved frequently, forcing Cruise to change schools fifteen times. His father was cold and distant. His parents divorced when Cruise was twelve years old, leaving him as the man of the house, forced to take on adult responsibilities at a young age. Along with his sisters, he had to go to work to help support the family during his early teens. Cruise also had difficulties in school because of a learning disability.

Yet Tom Cruise did not let life's difficulties slow him down. Instead, he transformed the pain and turbulence of his childhood into a steely determination to be the best. Even when the odds were stacked against him, Tom Cruise knew that hard work and dedication could make his dreams come true.

Humble Beginnings

Thomas Cruise Mapother IV was born on July 3, 1962, in Syracuse, New York. His parents—Thomas Cruise Mapother III and his wife, Mary Lee Pfeiffer—already had two daughters, Lee Anne and Marian. A few years later, a third daughter, Cass, would complete the family.

Cruise's mother, Mary Lee, was a loving, lively woman who did her best to keep the family together during its troubled times.

Cruise in 1981, the year he got his first big break. Growing up, Cruise faced many difficulties, including his parents' divorce and a learning disability.

She was close to her children and always ready to encourage their adventurous spirits. When Cruise was about two years old, he liked to wander out of the house and explore. Rather than scold the child for misbehaving, Mary Lee told him that the next time he wanted to go on an adventure, he should tell her so she could join him.

Thomas Cruise Mapother III was an engineer at General Electric. Cruise's father was extremely smart and creative; Cruise later described him as "complex, extremely bright, artistic."[1]

But the elder Mapother was more devoted to his work than to his family. He spent long hours developing new laser technologies for General Electric and took little interest in his children or his wife. His job also called for him to move around the country frequently to work on new research projects. That meant his family was constantly being uprooted and moved to a new home in a new town.

Even when the elder Mapother was around, the relationship between father and son was strained. The father simply was not very interested in his son's life or accomplishments. He rarely attended school or social events in which his son took part. Cruise's father was also more focused on his own feelings and interests, rather than anyone else's. Cruise recalled a time when he and his father had been driving for a long time in the car, and Cruise complained that he was hungry and wanted something to eat. But his father was not hungry, so he refused to stop.

In an interview with Tom Friend in *Premiere* magazine, Cruise recalled the violent games of catch he played with his father when he was nine years old. Cruise explained that his father tried to teach him how to catch a baseball by throwing it at sixty-five miles per hour at the boy's unprotected body:

> Well, every kid's a little afraid of that hardball when you go from T-ball to hardball. So, he'd take me out there— and this guy's six foot two—and he'd just start lightly with the ball, then just start *hammering* this baseball into my glove. The ball'd be bouncing off my head. . . . Sometimes if it hit my head, my nose would bleed and some tears would come up. He wasn't very comforting.[2]

After working for General Electric for many years, Tom Cruise's father decided that he could use his knowledge and experience to invent a new type of laser. He hoped this new invention would bring him fame and a lot of money. For the next twelve years, the Mapother family followed the father's dream across North America as he tried to market his invention. The family moved about every eighteen months, and each time, Cruise faced the challenge of trying to fit in at a new school.

Fitting In

By the time Tom Cruise started school, the family was living in Ottawa, Canada. The young boy got off to a rough start. He was the new kid in town and had to make new friends and find acceptance in a strange place.

Cruise had a reputation as a dreamer. He often got in trouble for failing to do his chores. It was not that he did not want to do them—often, he simply got distracted and forgot all about the job he was supposed to be doing. Cruise later said,

> I was always the kid who forgot to take the garbage out on Tuesdays. I would be in the backyard staring at the clouds, daydreaming. I was the kind of kid who wanted adventure. I craved it. I'd go around the backyard, dreaming up monsters and dragons. It was all about needing adventure. I had an active imagination. My mother thought, If you have all this imagination, why can't you take out the garbage![3]

Cruise's family learned to live with his daydreams and wild imagination. But when Cruise went to school, he faced a whole new set of problems—and teachers and students who were not as able or willing to put up with him. It soon became obvious that academics were not Cruise's strong point. He had so much trouble with reading, writing, and spelling that he was labeled a slow learner by his teachers. This led to endless teasing from his classmates. In 1985, Cruise recalled what his school days were like: "Reading before the class was the most frustrating thing for me . . . I felt like I was dumb. I was real embarrassed . . . my teachers were upset with me."[4]

It turned out that Cruise's academic problems were caused not by low intelligence, but by dyslexia, a learning disability. Cruise's mother and sisters also struggled with this disorder, and his mother proved to be an ally in helping him deal with it. She not only had the condition herself, but she also taught dyslexic children. She was able to help Cruise and his sisters master techniques to overcome the disability. Cruise found it especially helpful to create mental pictures to focus his attention and help him understand what he read.

A Family Divided

Cruise's life at home was not much better. His father's devotion to his work led to many long absences, broken promises, and missed family events. But his father's dream of success never came true. Instead, it broke up the family altogether.

In time, Mary Lee ran out of patience with her husband's lifestyle, and she was unable to tolerate the conditions of her marriage. In 1974, when Tom Cruise was twelve years old, the Mapother parents sat down with their four children and told them the news: They were getting divorced.

Thomas Mapother III had very little contact with his children after the divorce and never gave them any financial support.

What Is Dyslexia?

Dyslexia is a neurological condition that distorts the way printed words or numerals appear. The term comes from two Greek words, *dys*, meaning "difficulty," and *lexis*, meaning "words." A person with dyslexia may see letters backward or jumbled up. Often, a dyslexic is unable to tell whether a letter curves to the right or to the left. That makes it hard to tell the difference between, for example, the letters *b* and *d*.

Because dyslexics have trouble understanding words and sentences, they cannot learn to read or write in the same way others do. Even though dyslexics are usually above average in intelligence, they are often considered stupid at first because they have difficulty with basic academic subjects.

There is no cure for dyslexia. Instead, people with this condition must compensate by studying harder, learning material in a new way, or using mental strategies to remember how letters and words look.

Like Cruise, this student has dyslexia, a neurological condition that often causes sufferers to see letters backward or jumbled up.

Among the children, Cruise was especially resentful and angry about his father's neglect. Cruise dealt with his feelings by pretending his father simply did not exist anymore. One of his neighbors recalled that "it was as if his father had been wiped from the face of the earth."[5] As soon as he turned eighteen, Thomas Cruise Mapother IV dropped his father's last name. From then on, he would be known as Tom Cruise.

In 1983, as Cruise was just beginning his rise to stardom, his father told a reporter that he had "made a personal decision to respect my son's wishes, which was for me to stay the hell out of everything."[6] Cruise did see his father before the older man died of cancer in 1984. Cruise and his sisters surprised their dad by visiting him in the hospital. Cruise came away from that emotional meeting with more information about his father's reasons for abandoning the family. And he realized that his father was indeed sorry for not having been part of his children's lives. Although the meeting brought Cruise some peace, he never really lost the sense of anger and confusion over the events of his childhood.

Cruise has always had a close relationship with his mother, Mary Lee (pictured).

After the divorce, Mary Lee took the children and moved back to Louisville, Kentucky, her hometown. The family struggled financially. Mary Lee worked as many as four jobs at once to support her four children. The children worked too. Cruise's sisters were waitresses; Cruise himself mowed lawns and delivered newspapers to help make ends meet. One year, money was so scarce that the family could not afford to buy Christmas presents. Instead, they wrote poems and read them to each other in place of exchanging gifts. At one point, Mary Lee was almost forced to apply for food stamps to feed her family. But her sense of pride would not allow her to ask for help. Instead, she and her children simply worked harder to survive.

During these difficult times, Cruise was very protective of his mother. "When I hear about a mom who is single, my heart goes right there,"[7] Cruise told *People* magazine in 1999. One of the worst moments came when Mary Lee's boss at an appliance store asked her to move a washing machine by herself. Mary Lee hurt her back so badly that she was in traction for eight months, and a friend of the family had to move in to help out. Cruise told *Premiere* magazine that Mary Lee's boss "was not a good guy. He didn't pay for it, said it was my mother's fault. . . . My mother's not a bitter person, but I remember just being very, very angry about that."[8]

Cruise's protectiveness extended to his sisters. In a 1996 interview, he recalled how his sisters used to bring their boyfriends home for his approval. Cruise was quick to let these boys know that he would not allow his sisters to be hurt. He recalls,

> My sister Mary couldn't figure out for years why this guy wouldn't kiss her. Well, because I told him not to. The guy was a year older than me, but I said, "If you kiss my sister, I'm going to kill you, man. I'll kill you." Because I knew he had another girlfriend.[9]

To this day, Cruise is still very close to his mother and sisters. He credits his relationships with them for helping him understand and respect women.

During his early teen years, Cruise was very lonely. He later told an interviewer,

> After a divorce, you feel so vulnerable. And traveling the way I did, you're closed off a lot from other people. I didn't express a lot to people where I moved. They didn't have the childhood I had, and I didn't feel like they'd understand me. I was always warming up, getting acquainted with everyone. I went through a period, after the divorce, of really wanting to be accepted, wanting love and attention from people. But I never really seemed to fit in anywhere.[10]

Life was not all grim for the family, however. Cruise entertained his family by imitating television characters and putting on funny shows. He also credits his mother's optimistic attitude for giving him a positive outlook on life, despite its setbacks. As he explained to *Talk* magazine's Chris Connelly:

> There have been times in my life when I've been really, really unhappy, and most of that happened when I was very young. Painfully miserable at times. I would have moments of that, days of that, but I've not been a depressed kind of person. That's not who I am.
>
> I think also my mother was huge in that way. For her the cup was always half full. Always. And I loved her for it. She had that kind of impact on us. Things were tough. . . . And she wasn't perfect. I'm not saying that, but she was batting better than .500. . . . She definitely would have been on the All-Star team.[11]

Cruise spent most of what little money he had on movies. He saw *Star Wars* fourteen times and calls the World War II classic *Midway* his favorite action film. "You go early [to the multiplex] and figure out the times," he explained to *People* magazine. "Then you pay for one movie and figure out how you can sneak into all the other ones. That was my life of crime."[12] Later, after his movies had drawn tremendous audiences into movie theaters, Cruise joked about his huge success, saying, "I certainly paid them back for all the movies I saw that way."[13]

High School

In 1976, Cruise began high school at St. Francis Seminary in Cincinnati, Ohio, about one hundred miles north of Louisville. Cruise's family was Roman Catholic, and he received a scholarship to attend the all-boys' boarding school. Cruise had expressed interest in becoming a priest, although his friends and family doubted he was really serious about such a life-changing decision. Cruise had only been at the school a few weeks before he realized that he missed girls too much to seriously consider life as a priest. He also found being away from home—and his mother and sisters—very hard.

As a child Cruise loved to go to movies. He saw the 1977 blockbuster Star Wars *(above) fourteen times.*

Despite feeling homesick and out of place, Cruise found there were some good things about life at St. Francis. The school had only about one hundred students, and the small class size meant that he was finally able to receive the individual attention he needed to overcome his dyslexia. For the first time in his life, Cruise did well academically. Another aspect of St. Francis that appealed to Cruise was its athletic program. The school boasted a swimming pool, tennis courts, and many playing fields. Cruise played several school sports, including baseball, basketball, football, and lacrosse.

After completing his freshman year at St. Francis, Cruise decided not to return. He knew he had received a good education at the school, but he had also decided against becoming a priest. Besides, he was ready to rejoin his family. So he went home to Louisville to attend St. Xavier High School. He discovered a big change had occurred while he was away. His mother was dating a man named Jack South. At first, Cruise was jealous of South's involvement in their lives. For many years, it had been just Cruise and his mother and sisters. Now a stranger had entered their tight

Cruise (front row, far right) as a football player in All the Right Moves. *Cruise briefly played football in high school, but was too small to excel in the sport.*

family circle. But in time, Cruise realized how well South treated his mother and how happy she was to be with him. In the spring of Cruise's tenth-grade year, Jack South and Mary Lee Pfeiffer were married.

His mother's remarriage gave the family emotional and financial stability. But it also uprooted them yet again. Shortly after the wedding, the family moved to Glen Ridge, New Jersey. Once more, Cruise was the new kid at school, beginning his junior year at Glen Ridge High School in 1978. Friends recall him as being shy but fun, and a nice guy to be around.

One of the first things Cruise did was join the football team. Although he was too small to be a football star—just five feet seven inches and less than 125 pounds—Cruise worked hard to be the best player he could.

After football season ended, he joined the wrestling team. Again, he did not stand out on the team, but he gave his best effort. Cruise always practiced hard and followed his coach's instructions. He seemed determined to make up for a lack of talent with sheer hard work.

Cruise's wrestling career didn't last long. One day, while running to lose a few pounds to make his weight class, Cruise fell on some stairs and pulled the tendons in both knees. The injury was serious enough to knock him off the wrestling team. It also changed the course of his life.

A New Passion

Without sports to keep him occupied, Cruise was bored. He decided to fill his time by auditioning for the school musical, *Guys and Dolls*. Cruise won the lead role of gangster Nathan Detroit.

The role required Cruise to learn a lot of dialogue and sing several songs. Cruise's dyslexia made memorizing the script a challenge. As he had with sports, Cruise set about overcoming this challenge by working hard. He spent hours going over the script and the music, focusing all his energy on learning the part and bringing the character of Nathan Detroit to life.

From the moment Cruise stepped onstage on opening night, he was hooked by the sound of the audience's applause. After the show was over, the praise for his natural acting ability made Cruise

The Lure of New York

New York City has long been a mecca for people hoping to make a living in the performing arts. Although Los Angeles is better known as the center of the movie and television industries, New York also has a strong presence in these fields. Many movies and television shows are filmed in New York City, and a number of studios and production companies are located there. The city is home to large number of movie and television stars, giving New York a glamorous reputation.

It is also the center of the theatrical world. Broadway shows are a major feature of New York's entertainment scene, and the city is also home to many off-Broadway and other professional theaters. In addition, performers can show off their talents in the city's many comedy clubs, cabarets, and nightclubs. Several major opera companies and dance troupes also call New York City home.

Numerous young people come to this city to start modeling careers because many well-known talent and modeling agencies have offices there. Most of the major fashion magazines are based in New York as well.

The city is also home to two of the best-known drama schools in the United States, the American Academy of Dramatic Arts and the Juilliard School of Music. In addition, a number of smaller schools, programs, and workshops teach acting, music, dance, and other performing arts. And the city's large size means there are plenty of jobs, such as waitressing or working as office assistants or store clerks, to help aspiring actors pay the rent. All these reasons make New York the place to be for many who hope to become professional performers.

New York City is a mecca for people hoping to break into the entertainment industry.

feel excited, proud, and happy. "I felt I needed to act the way I needed air to breathe,"[14] he later said.

Cruise was even more excited when a show business agent who happened to be in the audience came backstage and told Cruise he had a natural talent for acting. When he came home that night, he announced to his mother and stepfather that acting was what he wanted to do with the rest of his life.

Cruise's mother and stepfather were less than thrilled about their son's choice of career. They knew that acting was a difficult profession to break into and the odds against becoming successful were astronomical. But Cruise was determined. As with every other challenge in his life, he was confident that if he worked hard, he would succeed. Cruise asked his parents to give him their blessing and ten years to see if he could make a living as an actor. Finally, they agreed and loaned Cruise $850 to get started.

Cruise was so eager to start his acting career that he skipped his high school graduation ceremony. As his classmates were receiving their diplomas and getting ready to head off to college, Tom Cruise was starting a new life in New York City. It was time to find an agent and set about the business of acting.

Chapter 2

Early Struggles and Successes

TOM CRUISE ARRIVED in New York City in the summer of 1980. He was seventeen years old and had $2,000 in his pocket—money he had saved from various part-time jobs, plus the $850 loan from his parents. He was about to follow the path taken by thousands of other aspiring actors. It was time to hire a manager to guide his career, audition for acting roles, and find a job to pay the rent.

Cruise's talent was obvious to many in the business, and he quickly found a manager to represent him. Within five months, he had won his first movie role, a bit part in the teen love story *Endless Love.*

Struggling to Survive

Cruise was on-screen for just a few minutes in *Endless Love,* playing the role of the main character's friend. He made only about three hundred dollars for his one-day job. That certainly was not enough to pay the bills, especially in an expensive city like New York. So, like other young actors before him, Cruise found jobs as a waiter and busboy. He attended acting classes during the day, worked at night, and went to every audition he could find.

One actor who met Cruise in those days described him as "very New Jersey, less polished than he is now . . . he was like a greaser—he had big muscles, he had his hair greased back. He had an angry edge to him."[15] But as journalist Chris Connelly later explained, "Those who saw him then recall an urgency in his performing that was hard to dismiss."[16] In fact, Cruise struck everyone as being totally focused and single-minded about succeeding as an actor.

Cruise found several ways to live cheaply. He found a roommate to split the rent on his apartment. For a while, he worked as a handyman and assistant building superintendent in exchange for living rent-free. He hitchhiked home to Glen Ridge for some of his mother's home cooking. He also slept on friends' floors. One of

Cruise's first movie role was in the film Endless Love *starring Brooke Shields.*

those friends was Emilio Estevez, another young actor who would go on to Hollywood stardom.

Tom Cruise's Big Break

Finally, in May 1981, less than a year after he came to New York, Cruise got his first big break when he auditioned for a movie called *Taps*. The movie told the story of a confrontation between students at a military school and the local police. Cruise was hired for a small role as one of the leading character's friends. Even though he had only a small part, Cruise threw himself into the work. He lifted weights, worked out, and drank milkshakes to put on fifteen pounds of muscle.

The director, Harold Becker, noticed Cruise's dedication and decided he deserved a bigger role. At first, he tried to make Cruise's small role into a bigger part. But there was no way to make that work. Finally, Becker asked Cruise if he would like to replace the actor who had been cast as David Shawn, the trigger-happy student leader.

At first, Cruise was embarrassed by the idea of what seemed like stealing another actor's part. To him, doing so would be rude, pushy, and unprofessional. He explained later,

> I said, 'Thank you very much but I don't want to play David Shawn.' I was in a small role and that's the way I wanted it to be. I was learning so much just being around, watching everything that was happening.[17]

However, others on the set did not agree with Cruise's polite modesty. Actor Sean Penn, who was also in the movie, recalled that,

> Tommy had to get the part. Very intense, 200 percent there. It was overpowering—and we'd all kind of laugh because it was so sincere. Good acting, but so far in the intense direction that it was funny. The producers told him, "Look, buddy, if you don't want to do it, leave. We want you for this part, but we're not going to beg you." It was incredible how innocent and naive he was when he came to do *Taps*.[18]

Cruise's hard work and dedication to his role in Taps *earned him the respect of Timothy Hutton (center) and Sean Penn (right).*

Cruise finally accepted the part.

Along with his costars, Cruise went to a Pennsylvania military academy to live the life of a cadet. Costar Timothy Hutton said that Cruise brought "such incredible confidence to his role that all our heads turned around. He worked incredibly hard."[19] Cruise took part in daily drills with weapons, marched in training parades, and learned every detail of military life. He loved the discipline and hard work. He felt that it was important to become the character if he was to give a believable performance. After the film's release, Cruise told an interviewer,

> To make the character as real as possible I have to find out how I can relate to the character personally. I have to find out what is "real" in the character that I do . . . there are going to be some points where you're going to have to be like a part of the character in terms of yourself, or else your character won't be real.[20]

Taps won a lot of attention for Cruise, Hutton, and Penn. The movie received mixed reviews but was financially successful. Tom Cruise had taken the first step to Hollywood stardom. But the pressures of playing such an intense character took their toll on the young actor. After the movie finished shooting, Cruise retreated to

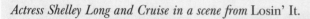

Actress Shelley Long and Cruise in a scene from Losin' It.

his grandfather's log cabin in Kentucky to unwind. He was so emotionally drained that he found it hard to stop acting aggressive and
psychotic in real life; it was almost as if he could not separate himself from the role of David Shawn. Later, Cruise admitted that right
after *Taps* he was "the most unpleasant person to be around."[21]

Cruise also spent his vacation in Kentucky thinking about his
career. When he returned, he told his agent that he did not want
to audition for any commercials or television roles. There was only
one thing he wanted to do: make movies.

A Losing Experience

On the advice of his agent, Cruise chose a role in a film called
Losin' It as a follow-up to his successful role in *Taps*. Cruise had his
doubts about the film from the start because he felt the script was
badly written, but his agent and the producers pushed him to appear in it. He recalled being told "Don't worry about the script
right now; we're going to work on it."[22] But the script was not
changed and *Losin' It*—a comedy about four teenagers and their
wild weekend in Tijuana—was a critical and commercial disaster.

Just as he had taken the troubles of his childhood and transformed them into a fierce will to succeed, Cruise learned from his
bad experience in *Losin' It*. He fired his agent and decided that in
the future, he would never take a role that he did not think was
good for him or his career.

> It was a real eye-opener. It made me understand how you
> really have to be careful . . . you've got to examine all the
> elements of a project. I learned a great lesson in doing that
> movie. I realized that I'd have to learn how to survive in
> this business and not let it eat me up. I knew that the kinds
> of films I wanted to work on from then on had to be made
> by the best people. There I was, with the opportunity to be
> a working actor and I remember thinking that this wasn't
> going to last forever. Money was never a factor with me—
> I wanted to learn on a film. Money goes, but what you
> learn can't be taken away from you. Even though the film
> wasn't as bad as it could have been, it still wasn't the kind
> I wanted to be involved with.[23]

Francis Ford Coppola

Francis Ford Coppola is one of America's most respected and admired film-makers. He was born in Detroit, Michigan, in 1939 and studied film at the University of California at Los Angeles. While he was at film school, he began working with Roger Corman, a well-known producer of low-budget movies. Coppola directed his first feature film, *December 13*, in 1963. Also a writer of screenplays, he later won an Oscar® for the screenplay of *Patton*, a biography of the World War II general.

Coppola achieved his biggest success in 1972, when he directed *The Godfather*. This portrait of a family's involvement in the American Mafia is considered a masterpiece. It was the biggest box office success of its time and won an Oscar® for best picture. Coppola was also nominated for best director. In 1974, he continued the story in *The Godfather II*, which became the first (and so far, the only) sequel to win an Oscar® for best picture. Coppola won a best director Oscar® for the film. In 1990, he completed the saga with *The Godfather III*, which received nominations for best picture and best director.

Coppola also received a best director nomination for his 1979 film *Apocalypse Now*, a look at America's role in the Vietnam War. In addition, he has produced a number of other well-known films, including such children's favorites as *The Black Stallion* (1979) and *The Secret Garden* (1993).

A Smart Move

Cruise's next role would team him with director Francis Ford Coppola for the movie *The Outsiders*, based on the classic novel by S. E. Hinton. Coppola was a legend in Hollywood, highly respected for his work on *The Godfather, The Godfather II,* and *Apocalypse Now.* Cruise was so eager to work with the director that he told him, "Look, I don't care what role you give me. I really want to work with you. I want to be there on the set and watch. I'll do anything it takes; I'll play any role in this."[24]

Cruise ended up with the small part of Steve Randle, a tough gang member from a broken home. To make himself look like a rough, tough teen, Cruise had a cap removed from one of his front teeth and also refused to shower during most of the nine-week shoot. "I work very hard," Cruise said of his devotion to becoming part of his characters. "My craft is the most important thing in my life."[25]

Coppola was so impressed with the young actor's work on the film that he offered Cruise a part in his next film, *Rumble Fish,* which was also based on an S. E. Hinton novel. But Cruise had to turn down Coppola's offer. He had already signed up to do another movie, one that would change his life and career. It was called *Risky Business.*

Shooting to the Top

Risky Business told the story of Joel Goodsen, a rich kid who has always played by the rules. But when Joel's parents go out of town for the weekend, the teenager breaks free from his goody-two-shoes image.

Cruise (far right) played a tough gang member in the Francis Ford Coppola movie The Outsiders.

As events spiral out of control, Joel is transformed from a dutiful son into a wild party animal—who nevertheless wins both the girl and a promising future as he gets away with all sorts of mischief and mayhem.

The part of Joel Goodsen was Tom Cruise's first leading movie role, and the critics were especially impressed with his performance. Critic Roger Ebert enthused, "He occupies this movie the way Dustin Hoffman occupied *The Graduate*,"[26] comparing Cruise's performance to one in the 1967 movie masterpiece. *Risky Business* was a huge commercial success as well, and audiences flocked to theaters to see this new film.

One of the funniest and most memorable scenes in the movie featured Cruise dancing in his underwear and a dress shirt, using a candlestick for a microphone, as the song "Old Time Rock 'n' Roll" blasted away in the background. This scene, which became a classic, was completely improvised by Cruise. As he explained to *People* magazine's David Hutchings shortly after the film's release, "With kids, to be a rock star is the ultimate. When their parents leave, they turn the music up. Dancing with your pants off—it's total freedom."[27] This scene, along with Cruise's charm and good looks, helped make *Risky Business* a huge hit and catapulted Cruise into the front ranks of Hollywood's sex symbols.

First Love

Risky Business brought something to Cruise besides fame and fortune. During the course of the film, he began dating his costar, Rebecca De Mornay. At first, the two had trouble working together because Cruise found it hard to act romantically toward his beautiful young costar as the script demanded. Soon, however, the two were dating steadily. De Mornay became Cruise's first serious girlfriend.

However, the relationship taught Cruise that Hollywood romances have their downside. Cruise and De Mornay were followed everywhere by tabloid photographers and reporters (known as *paparazzi*) looking for a story. Soon the couple was front-page news, and stories and photos about them appeared in many magazines and newspapers. Cruise hated this invasion of privacy, es-

The film Risky Business *catapulted Cruise to stardom. During filming, Cruise began dating his costar, Rebecca De Mornay (pictured).*

pecially since the stories about the romance were not always true. Several years after they began dating, the couple broke up. But Cruise's annoyance at the media would continue throughout his career.

Keeping Actors Safe: The Role of Stuntpeople

When you watch a movie, it may look like the actors are putting themselves in all sorts of dangerous situations, such as elaborate fight scenes, wild car chases, violent natural disasters, or grueling sporting events. The truth is that actors rarely take part in these physically punishing scenes. Instead, their roles are played by stuntmen and stunt women.

People who do stunts are specially trained. Many of them have studied martial arts and know how to stage a fight so that it looks real, without anyone actually suffering physical injuries. Other stuntpeople are professional athletes who have spent years toughening up their bodies to endure the physical abuse of their jobs. Stuntpeople who stage car chases or fly helicopters or airplanes are specially trained to perform these dangerous feats safely. Doing stunts requires a lot of courage, along with knowledge and experience.

When a risky scene is being filmed, the actor takes part in as much of the filming as possible, without putting his or her life in danger. Then a stuntperson steps in to finish the job and act in scenes that are very dangerous or require special knowledge to perform. Usually, the scene will be filmed in such a way that the viewer doesn't see enough of the character to realize the actor is not on-screen. For example, a movie might show an actor in a car that is about to crash. But the crash itself will be filmed from outside the car, so the driver—now being played by a stuntman rather than the actor—is not visible. After the crash, the actor goes back into the scene to film what happens next. The viewer is tricked into thinking that the actor was in every scene.

Today, computer-generated images sometimes take the place of stuntpeople. Filmmakers can use computers to create images of characters and insert them into dangerous or dramatic scenes. They can also create images of the lead actors. This practice helps reduce the risk of injury or death and also helps create an even stronger illusion on film.

Cruise also found reporters' questions about his past and his personal life hard to answer. No one had prepared him for the intensity of being a star, and he felt uncomfortable about being in the spotlight twenty-four hours a day. He did not feel the public would be that impressed by his opinions or his personal life. He once described his discomfort at being stared at in public by saying, "I used to think . . . is something hanging out of my nose? It took time to get adjusted to it."[28]

Good and Bad Choices

Cruise followed up his success in *Risky Business* with a pair of very different films. First he starred in *All the Right Moves* as Stefan Djorjevic, a boy struggling to escape the poverty of his hometown by becoming a football star. Cruise identified with the character of Stefan because he too had struggled to escape poverty. But Cruise also noted, "I think on certain levels I could identify with the guy. But I didn't need the ticket out. I didn't feel that trapped."[29]

Once again, Cruise threw himself into his role. He worked out to build up his muscles and used memories of his days as a high school football player to make his character seem realistic. He also insisted on taking part in the football scenes, rather than using a stuntman for the action. Cruise played so roughly that he even suffered a mild concussion while filming a scene for the movie.

Cruise also made an impression on the script for *All the Right Moves*. He had a good working relationship with the film's director, Michael Chapman. The two met many times at Chapman's house

Director Michael Chapman gives pointers to Cruise for a scene in All The Right Moves.

to go over the script. Cruise rewrote some of the dialogue so that it better expressed his character's feelings. As journalist Wensley Clarkson noted in his biography of Cruise, the young actor believed that "he was the one who would be damaged by sloppy dialogue and he was determined to ensure that every word he spoke would be completely believable."[30]

All the Right Moves was not as big a hit as *Risky Business*, but Cruise received excellent reviews for his portrayal of Stefan. Unfortunately, Cruise's next movie, *Legend*, would be one of the low points of his career. A fantasy about a quest to save a unicorn, the film was plagued with disasters. A fox that Cruise had to hold during one scene badly scratched his legs, and Cruise also injured his back halfway through the filming. Worst of all, most of the set burned down in a raging fire one day while the cast was at lunch. This disaster led to a long delay in the shooting schedule while sets were rebuilt.

Through all the difficulties, Cruise gritted his teeth and tried to do his best:

> I really had to make a choice. When the set burned down, it was like, "What are we going to do now? Where does this take us?" I said, "I can sit here and . . . wallow in my frustration" and banging your head against the wall, you say, "Okay, that happened, now what do we do? Let's go ahead." . . . I mean, I always had that ability to just deal with things. My whole life has been like that: "OK, what do I do now?"[31]

Despite his hard work, the film seemed fated to fail. Cruise wore long hair and tights to play his fairy-tale character, Jack 'o the Green, and audiences and critics thought he looked ridiculous. The movie bombed, and many were sure Cruise's career was finished. But he was about to film a movie that would shoot his popularity straight to the top.

Top Gun

While he was still filming *Legend*, Cruise read a script for a movie called *Top Gun*, which was about Navy fighter pilots. The film's producers, Jerry Bruckheimer and Don Simpson, wanted Cruise to

Cruise as Jack o' the Green in the box office disaster Legend. *Many thought the movie would ruin Cruise's blossoming career.*

play Pete "Maverick" Mitchell, a hotshot fighter pilot who is determined to be the best at the Navy training school and who eventually becomes a hero in a fierce aerial fight with enemy pilots.

Cruise was interested in playing Maverick, but he felt the script needed work. He told Bruckheimer, Simpson, and director Tony Scott that he wanted to rewrite the script to develop his character more fully:

The Real Top Guns

The movie *Top Gun* was based on a real program for fighter pilots then located at Miramar Naval Air Station in San Diego, California. (The program has since moved to Fallen Naval Air Station in Nevada.) One of the movie's producers, Jerry Bruckheimer, had read an article about this flight school for the U.S. Navy's best fighter pilots. He immediately knew the story of these pilots would make a great movie.

The Top Gun pilots are chosen for the program on the basis of their ability and achievements. Only the best pilots have a chance of getting in. They have to be in top shape, both physically and psychologically. They have to know how to fly a variety of aircraft, enjoy flying more than anything else, and not be afraid to live life on the edge.

Top Gun pilots must learn to withstand the high G-forces (forces of gravity) created by violent flying maneuvers. These G-forces put incredible pressure on the human body. Pilots also learn how to eject from a plane and how to survive crash landings in water and on land.

A scene from the 1986 blockbuster Top Gun, *which was based on a real flight school that produces top U.S. Navy fighter pilots.*

It was important to me that we made a movie about characters and the human element—not just a war picture. I've got a strong point of view and I like to get it across in the films I do. Everything that I've done to get involved in this was to benefit the piece itself.[32]

Scott, Bruckheimer, and Simpson were a bit startled by Cruise's bold demands. But they wanted him in their movie, and they also agreed that the script needed work. Finally, the producers gave Cruise two months to work on the script and develop his character before signing a contract to be in the movie.

Cruise later recalled his boldness in an interview with *Talk* magazine's Chris Connelly. Responding to Connelly's comment that "You're talking to a guy who used to be president of production at Paramount, and you're saying, 'The character's not there. Maybe we could fix this,'" Cruise laughed and said:

> When I first made my deal for *Top Gun* . . . can you imagine this? I wasn't exactly the most mature-looking 23-year-old guy, either. . . . But sometimes those young guys are right, that's why you've got to make sure you listen to 'em. . . . I'm 23 years old—what balls! . . . Three years before that I was in New York busing tables or in high school.[33]

Top Gun went on to make more than 175 million and become the top movie of 1986. And it catapulted Tom Cruise to a new level of stardom. He was now the hottest actor of his generation. *People* magazine later described him this way:

> Cruise soon cornered the market on cocky hotshots who come to realize that the time for youthful mischief is over.

Before Cruise (right) would agree to play Maverick in Top Gun, *he insisted on rewriting the script in order to develop his character more fully.*

Tom Cruise Filmography

Endless Love (1981)

Taps (1982)

Losin' It (1983)

The Outsiders (1983)

Risky Business (1983)

All the Right Moves (1983)

Legend (1985)

Top Gun (1986)

The Color of Money (1987)

Cocktail (1988)

Rain Man (1988)

Born on the Fourth of July (1989)

Days of Thunder (1990)

Far and Away (1991)

A Few Good Men (1992)

The Firm (1993)

Interview with the Vampire (1994)

Mission: Impossible (1996)

Jerry Maguire (1996)

Eyes Wide Shut (1999)

Magnolia (1999)

Mission: Impossible II (2000)

The props change—Navy fighter planes in *Top Gun*, blenders in *Cocktail*, race cars in *Days of Thunder*. But the result is usually the same: victory.[34]

"This is the very beginning," Cruise told an interviewer in 1986. "I don't want to be the next James Dean. That's been done."[35] Cruise was comparing himself to an actor who had become a cult figure after he was killed in a car crash at the age of twenty-four, after making only three movies. Cruise had no intention of letting his stardom peak at such a young age. He had a lot more he wanted to accomplish, both in his professional and his personal life.

Chapter 3

Working with Giants

In 1986, CRUISE was at the height of his popularity with fans. But he did not want to be only a sex symbol or a celebrity; he considered himself a serious actor who was dedicated to his craft. And so he set about learning more about how to be a good actor by working with some of the best actors in the business.

Cruise followed his starring role in *Top Gun* with a supporting role in *The Color of Money*. This movie gave Cruise the opportunity

Cruise teamed up with acting legend Paul Newman to appear in the Martin Scorsese film The Color of Money.

Paul Newman

Paul Newman is one of the best-known actors in American movie history. He was born in Cleveland, Ohio, in 1925. He acted in school plays in high school and college and went on to study at the prestigious Yale School of Drama in Connecticut and the Actors Studio in New York City.

Newman appeared in several Broadway plays in the 1950s, but he is most widely known for his work in movies and on television. Some of his best work was done in the 1960s, when he starred in such movies as *The Hustler* (1961), *Sweet Bird of Youth* (1962), *Hud* (1963), *Cool Hand Luke* (1967), and *Butch Cassidy and the Sundance Kid* (1969). *Butch Cassidy* became the highest-grossing Western in movie history, a record it held for many years. Newman's costar was another popular actor, Robert Redford. In 1973, Newman and Redford teamed up again to play a pair of con men in the immensely popular movie *The Sting*, which won an Oscar® for best picture.

Although he was nominated for Oscars® many times, Newman didn't win the Best Actor award until his seventh nomination in 1986, when he starred in the sequel to *The Hustler*, *The Color of Money*. The year before, the Academy of Motion Picture Arts and Sciences (the organization that awards Oscars®) had presented him with an honorary award for his lifetime of work in movies.

Newman's wife, Joanne Woodward, is an accomplished actress in her own right. She won a Best Actress Oscar® in 1957 for *The Three Faces of Eve* and was nominated again in 1968 for *Rachel, Rachel* (which was directed by her husband), in 1973 for *Summer Wishes, Winter Dreams*, and in 1990 for *Mr. and Mrs. Bridge* (which co-starred her husband).

Newman is also well known for his charitable work. He has his own line of foods, called Newman's Own, and donates all the profits to various charities, including his Hole in the Wall Gang summer camp for children with cancer and other serious illnesses.

to work with two Hollywood legends, actor Paul Newman and director Martin Scorsese. *The Color of Money* was a sequel to the classic 1961 movie *The Hustler*, about the high-stakes world of pool playing. Cruise would play Vincent Lauria, a young man who was the protégé of Paul Newman's hustler, Fast Eddie Felson.

The role of Vincent Lauria required Cruise to play pool—something he had never done before. A professional pool player was hired to teach Cruise how to play, and the young actor quickly picked up the finer points of the game. Paul Newman, who already knew how to play pool, was impressed by Cruise's skill. "It took me a long time to get OK," the older actor said. "It took him very little time to get very good."[36]

Cruise also spent many hours in New York City's pool halls, observing the pool players and hustlers. This not only helped his playing skills, it also gave him ideas for how his character would behave and helped him make Vincent Lauria true to life.

Cruise found it thrilling to work with actors and directors he had long admired. "The thrill isn't gone," he told *People* magazine in 1999. "I remember seeing [Martin] Scorsese and all of a sudden there I am across from [Paul] Newman and [Gene] Hackman. It's still pretty trippy for me."[37]

Cruise and Newman became fast friends. Newman, who was thirty-seven years older than Cruise, served as a father figure and mentor to the younger actor. He was impressed by how hard the young actor worked and by his willingness to try something new to flesh out his character, even if it made him look silly. "He's prepared to hang himself on a meat hook," Newman told the media.

> He'll hang himself out to dry to seek something. He's not afraid of looking like a ninny. He doesn't protect himself or his ego. And he's a wonderful experimenter. . . . He has what he needs to be a good actor.[38]

Cruise returned Newman's professional admiration. And Cruise respected not only Newman's acting ability but also his life away from the set. "He lives a normal life. He's got several businesses, a wife, a family. That's good for me to see,"[39] Cruise noted. The young actor hoped to achieve the same stability in his own life.

Critics and audiences alike responded to *The Color of Money*. The film did well at the box office, and Paul Newman received the first Oscar® of his long career, winning the Best Actor Award for his portrayal of Fast Eddie. Although Cruise was not even nominated for a Best Supporting Actor Award for his role in the movie, he treasured a telegram that Newman sent him. In it, Newman expressed his disappointment over Cruise's lack of a nomination and said, "If I win, it's ours as much as mine because you did such a good job."[40] The telegram meant so much to Cruise that he had it framed and hung it on the wall of his apartment.

Tom Finds Love—and Then Heartbreak

Outside of his busy work schedule during the late 1980s, Cruise
found time for his personal life. On May 9, 1987, he married actress
Mimi Rogers. Besides working in the same industry, the two shared
similar backgrounds. Rogers' parents had also divorced when she

*Cruise and actress Mimi Rogers. The two married in 1987 and were
divorced three years later.*

was young, and she and her younger brother were raised by their father. The family moved many times during her childhood, and Rogers, like Cruise, had struggled to fit in as the new kid.

Cruise referred to his wife as his best friend. But despite their apparent happiness together, Cruise and Rogers found it hard to make the marriage work. Both were dedicated to their acting careers, and they spent a great deal of time apart as they worked on various movie projects. Rogers also found it difficult to be known as Mrs. Tom Cruise—her husband was much more famous than she was. In the end, the two drifted apart and were divorced in early 1990. As always when it came to his personal life, Cruise refused to discuss the details of their separation and insisted that his private life was private.

Rogers, however, was not as circumspect about the failure of the marriage. She was disappointed that the marriage had not worked out and believed that Cruise's sudden rise to stardom was the reason the couple had had problems. As Cruise became more popular, there were more people around to do his bidding. Rogers definitely felt that all this attention had made Cruise more demanding and determined to get his way, no matter what other people wanted.

Rogers also did not share Cruise's obsession with his career and with movies in general. Although she was an actress, she was interested in many more things besides making movies. She once told an interviewer, "I want to go through the whole Museum of Natural History and read everything. I love the gems and natural minerals exhibit and the whale. It always amazes me that something could be so big."[41] These simply were not interests that Cruise shared.

Another Powerful Role

Despite the problems they faced later on, Cruise and Rogers were happy in 1987. However, Cruise did not let his new marriage interfere with his work schedule. He quickly followed up his serious role in *The Color of Money* with a slight comedy called *Cocktail.* Even though the film was a critical disaster, Cruise defended his decision to be in it. He explained his thinking to Chris Connelly of *Talk* magazine:

In the romantic comedy Cocktail, *Cruise played a bartender. Disliked by critics, the film nevertheless did well at the box office.*

Just do what interests you. Do what interests you because you can't bet on the idea that something's going to be successful and use that as a means of gratification. I always felt that if I learned something—good or bad, right or wrong—I could justify the experience. You want the studio to make the money back. . . . And you have got a responsibility; if it is your movie you want to make the money back. . . . You've got to be committed. If people are only interested in the fame and celebrity of it, you can see how they lose their way. Because you don't know what movie is going to be a hit. You don't. You can't go for that; you have to go for the experience. That's what I enjoy.[42]

Even though critics hated *Cocktail,* audiences hurried to see it. The film made more than $70 million, and it was clear that people were eager to see Tom Cruise, even in a terrible film.

Cruise's next project was *Rain Man,* which co-starred legendary actor Dustin Hoffman. In *Rain Man,* Cruise played the part of con man Charlie Babbitt, while Hoffman portrayed his brother, Raymond, who suffers from a mental disorder called *autism.* Charlie initially befriends Raymond only to get his hands on his brother's multimillion-dollar inheritance, but the relationship transforms Charlie into a more mature, compassionate human being.

Dustin Hoffman had already agreed to play the part of Raymond when Cruise signed on to the project. Hoffman was known as a fiercely dedicated actor who would do just about anything to make his characters real. Like Cruise, he insisted on having input on the script and on how his character was presented. The film's director, Barry Levinson, was quick to explain how he expected to work with his two leading actors:

> If an actor wants everything to be the way he wants it to be, then it's best to say, "Look, get your own . . . movie and do it yourself." But if you are working on collaboration,

In Rain Man, *Cruise played a con man and the younger brother of an autistic savant, portrayed by Dustin Hoffman.*

that's terrific, because if you are exchanging ideas you may find a better one that takes you to a higher level. That's what gives you adrenaline; it's what drives you and stimulates you.[43]

From the start, Hoffman was impressed with Cruise's dedication and hard work. He recalled how Cruise would get up at 4:30 in the morning and put in long hours on the set, then go back in the evening to watch the dailies—the film of the day's shooting. "He was like a machine in that sense," Hoffman said. "There is a joy in achieving excellence. It's all about the work."[44]

Rain Man was a huge success, even though most people in Hollywood didn't expect the movie to make a lot of money. The director himself said, "I thought this would be a kind of offbeat piece, even if it did star Tom Cruise."[45] However, *Rain Man* turned out to be a blockbuster. It made more than $42 million in the first eigh-

Mark Johnson (left), Dustin Hoffman, and Barry Levinson (right) display their Oscars® for Rain Man. *Although Cruise was highly praised for his work in the film, he was not nominated for an Academy Award.*

teen days of its release and more than $156 million in its first five months in U.S. theaters. It grossed more than $500 million worldwide. *Rain Man* was a huge critical success as well, winning an Oscar® for best picture, along with Best Director for Barry Levinson and Best Actor for Dustin Hoffman.

Many people were surprised that Cruise was not nominated for his work in the film. Movie expert Edward Gross noted:

> The feeling of teamwork between the two [Hoffman and Cruise] is obvious in the finished film, for they work together like one complete individual. Hoffman won the Academy Award and the lion's share of the credit for his excellent performance as Raymond. It's disconcerting, however, to see that Cruise was not equally lauded. In his hands, Charlie Babbitt is a flesh-and-blood human being who goes through a 180-degree transformation due to contact with the brother he never knew existed. Never again would anyone doubt [Cruise's] abilities as an actor.[46]

By the end of 1988, Tom Cruise was America's number-one box office star. But even though he had achieved phenomenal success, he knew he still had a long career ahead of him. He reflected,

> People asked after *Rain Man*, "How are you going to match the success of that picture?" I said I can't live my life by what is going to make $20 or even $100 million. I don't know what is going to happen to my career. I am going to take a lot of risks and some of it is going to work and some of it is not going to work. Some of it will be trash and some of it, I hope, will be good. I make the decisions. I pick the scripts. I have only myself to blame if things don't work out. That is how I want to live my life. That is the way I set out to live it at the beginning.[47]

New Challenges

By the late 1980s, Tom Cruise was ready for something new. He had reached the top of the box office charts, won the respect of Hollywood's best directors and actors, and become a sex symbol for

In Born on the Fourth of July, *Cruise portrayed real-life Vietnam War veteran Ron Kovic.*

millions around the world. Cruise could have continued to play the same all-American hotshot parts as always. But he wanted more. He wanted to explore new challenges and use his talent in more unusual and demanding roles.

Born on the Fourth of July was just what Cruise was looking for. The movie was based on the true story of Ron Kovic, a gung-ho soldier paralyzed in the Vietnam War who became an antiwar activist. Kovic wrote a book about his experiences, and it was about to be turned into a movie directed by fellow Vietnam veteran Oliver Stone.

The project was a risky one for Cruise. His previous roles had all shown him as a handsome, clean-cut, high-achieving man. But the role of Ron Kovic would place Cruise in a wheelchair and show him in humiliating physical and emotional situations.

As usual, Cruise threw himself into his role. He went through rugged physical training to act out the battle scenes. He also endured rigorous filming in the tropical jungles of the Philippines. Then he lost weight in order to look sickly and weak as his character suffered through horrible conditions at veterans' hospitals. Cruise also spent weeks in a wheelchair in an attempt to understand what life was like for Kovic after his paralyzing injury.

Cruise's hard work and dedication paid off. He received excellent reviews for his portrayal of Ron Kovic, along with a Golden Globe Award for best actor and his first Oscar® nomination for best

The Golden Globes

Although the Oscars® are the famous awards of the movie industry, winning a Golden Globe Award is a triumph in an actor's career. The Golden Globes are presented by the Hollywood Foreign Press Association, a group of foreign journalists working in Los Angeles. During World War II, foreign journalists found it difficult to get reports back to their home countries in Europe; neither were they taken seriously by the American press or by the movie stars themselves. To overcome these problems, the journalists formed the Hollywood Foreign Press Association in 1943 and decided to give out their own awards.

The first Golden Globe Awards were presented in 1944 at an informal ceremony. The winners—Jennifer Jones for *The Song of Bernadette* and Paul Lukas for *The Watch on the Rhine*—received scrolls. Over the years, the award ceremony grew more elaborate, and many more awards were presented. In 1955, awards for television performances were added. Today, the ceremony includes thirteen awards for movies and eleven for television.

The Golden Globes are presented several months before the Oscars®, and many movies and performers who win Golden Globes go on to win Academy Awards (also known as Oscars®). But there are always differences and surprises. One major difference between the Golden Globes and the Oscars® is that there are separate categories for comedies and dramas in the Golden Globes, while these performers and movies compete against each other for the Oscars®.

Cruise displays his Golden Globe Award for best supporting actor in Magnolia.

actor. Although Cruise didn't win the Oscar®, Oliver Stone did win for best director and praised Cruise in his acceptance speech.

His performance in the role of Ron Kovic helped people see that Tom Cruise was more than a handsome Hollywood hunk. People now realized he was a versatile actor who could play many different types of characters. As Cruise explained it,

> I remember after *Taps* they said, "Okay, he's the psychotic kind of guy." After *Risky Business* they said, "Okay, we've got the teen comedy guy." And after *Top Gun* it was like, "O-kay!" Then when I decided—when I was lucky enough to get *Born on the Fourth of July* . . . I mean, now people go, "Oh, of course, he can act." But at the time people were going, "What's the matter with this guy?" [Because I wasn't playing another] *Top Gun* hero. But that's what's fun.[48]

Love in the Fast Lane

Cruise's next film had nothing in common with *Born on the Fourth of July*. This time, Cruise would not tackle any great social issues. Instead, his next film would be based on one of his favorite hob-

Cruise celebrates his Golden Globe Award for best actor in Born on the Fourth of July, *along with fellow winners Oliver Stone (right) for best director and Ron Kovic for best screenplay.*

Days of Thunder
*featured Cruise as race car
driver Cole Trickle.*

bies. Paul Newman, Cruise's costar in *The Color of Money*, had introduced Cruise to the sport of auto racing. Cruise fell in love with the thrills, challenges, and dangers of the high-speed sport. Now he decided to make a movie about it.

Jerry Bruckheimer and Don Simpson, who had produced *Top Gun*, were eager to produce Cruise's new film as well. Cruise wrote an outline for the script, but he had trouble finding a writer who could make the story complete. Finally, Cruise teamed up with noted screenwriter Robert Towne to create a script called *Days of Thunder*. Cruise was excited to work with Towne, who had written such classic movies as *Bonnie and Clyde, The Godfather,* and *Chinatown*.

> What's great about Bob Towne is that he just came in and understood the world. He focused on the piece. He liked these people. I remember after an hour—we had gone to a race track—he said, "I get it, Cruise. I know what you're talking about. This is fantastic." That was exciting.[49]

Cruise didn't want *Days of Thunder* to be just a movie about fast cars. He wanted the characters to come across as realistic, interesting people locked in life-or-death combat. Cruise referred to race-car driving as

> manipulating a vehicle with tremendous power around a track. The level of competition is driver-to-driver. It's modern-day gladiators. It's a war. There's a tremendous amount of dignity in the characters and in the people I've met just hanging around the circuit.[50]

Cruise also took an active role in the casting of the movie. He insisted that the female lead be played by a relatively unknown Australian actress named Nicole Kidman. Cruise had seen Kidman in a thriller called *Dead Calm* and was fascinated by the young actress's presence on-screen. Cruise was eager to work with the tall, red-haired, strikingly beautiful actress and decided she would be perfect to play the part of Dr. Claire Lewicki in *Days of Thunder.*

Despite Cruise's dedication to the project, filming *Days of Thunder* was difficult. Cruise, Towne, and director Tony Scott were dissatisfied with the script and constantly rewriting and polishing it. Bad weather slowed down production when heavy rain and freezing weather made racing scenes difficult to shoot. To make matters worse, the film's release date was moved up several months to the Fourth of July weekend of 1990 to take advantage of the holiday crowds. That meant that Scott had just six weeks to edit the film and get it ready for audiences.

Cruise was also involved in editing the movie, and spent long hours on post-production duties. He found production work "exciting because it really puts you absolutely to the limit,"[51] he said. He was so focused that Simpson and Bruckheimer nicknamed him Laserhead. Cruise explained his devotion to his work this way:

> When I'm making a film, it's a year out of my life. I mean, I've been working on *Days of Thunder* for a year and a half, really, and for a year straight of seven days a week. So you have to believe in what you're doing and love it, because there are sacrifices. When I do something, I have to feel 100 percent committed.[52]

Although *Days of Thunder* received mostly bad reviews, it was a commercial success, earning a respectable $83 million. But for Cruise, the movie was significant in another way. On Christmas Eve 1990, Tom Cruise and his costar, Nicole Kidman, were married in the presence of their families and closest friends in Aspen, Colorado.

Nicole Kidman's Film Career

Although not as big a star as her husband, Nicole Kidman has a flourishing acting career. She was well known in Australia thanks to appearances in many miniseries and television shows. Her starring role in the Australian movie *Dead Calm* brought her to the attention of Hollywood. In the film, Kidman and her costar, Sam Neill, play a couple who are attacked and terrorized by an intruder on their yacht.

Kidman moved to California after her success in *Dead Calm*. Soon afterward, she was cast in *Days of Thunder* and later married the film's star, Tom Cruise. Along with appearing with her husband in several movies, Kidman won great critical success as the attention-hungry television weather reporter who plots her husband's murder in the 1995 film *To Die For*. She also appeared on stage in London and New York in the provocative play *The Blue Room*.

Cruise insisted on casting Nicole Kidman as the female lead in Days of Thunder *after seeing her in* Dead Calm *(pictured).*

While filming Days of Thunder, *Cruise fell in love with his costar, Nicole Kidman. The couple married on Christmas Eve, 1990.*

Kidman has said, "When I met Tom, he was a big star, he was young, and he wasn't happy."[53] Cruise agrees with Kidman's observation and claims his relationship with her has helped him relax and find balance in his life. He told *Vanity Fair* in 1996,

> In the beginning, I was always afraid. "This is my one shot. I'm going to lose it, so I've just gotta *work, work, work.*" The first 10 years . . . that was it, *work, work, work.* And then I met Nic, and it was like "Oh, my God." You read about people whose whole life is just movies and it's very small. Your life feeds your work, not the opposite. It's not about me, me, me, me. It's about the other person.[54]

Tom Cruise had found his soul mate in Nicole Kidman. His personal life was flourishing. And Cruise was determined to make sure his professional life was just as satisfying and on track.

Chapter 4

Taking Control

Duration THE EARLY 1990s, Cruise continued playing young men who overcome obstacles to become heroes. He and Nicole Kidman costarred as Irish immigrants in *Far and Away*; he went on to play lawyers in his next two films, *A Few Good Men* and *The Firm*.

Legal Difficulties

The legal terms in the scripts for *A Few Good Men* and *The Firm* were especially challenging for Cruise because of his dyslexia. But

Jack Nicholson and Cruise in A Few Good Men. *Mastering the legal terms in the script was especially challenging for Cruise because of his dyslexia.*

he overcame this obstacle as he had others in his life, by working harder. Kevin Bacon, who costarred in *A Few Good Men,* also had trouble learning his lines. The two actors spent a lot of time together studying their scripts and soon became friends. "It [the legal terminology] was completely foreign to me and, to a certain extent, to him," Bacon explained. "It was exhausting, but fun. That's why you act."[55] *A Few Good Men* and *The Firm* did well with both critics and audiences. Cruise was now earning $15 million per picture, which made him one of Hollywood's highest-paid stars.

Besides pleasing audiences, Cruise continued to impress directors and other actors. Sydney Pollack, who directed *The Firm,* remembers Cruise standing behind him during auditions for the female lead in that movie "so he could eavesdrop on everything that was said. He was working, studying the director's role."[56] Pollack also said that "having Tom in your movie is like having a great collaborator. It's wonderful to watch his dedication to the work."[57]

Pollack encouraged Cruise to try his own hand at directing. He asked Cruise to direct "The Frightening Frammies," an episode of Pollack's *Fallen Angels* series on the cable network Showtime in 1993. Series producer William Hornberg described Cruise as being "a little self-conscious. . . . You know, 'Here I am, the star, giving you your directions,' but he went into it with the appropriate sense of humor."[58]

"The Frightening Frammies" received good reviews when it appeared on Showtime in September 1993. But biographer Wensley Clarkson noted that Cruise

> later admitted that he had found the entire directing experience far from easy and voiced his delight at having chosen a relatively simple debut project as opposed to directing something as heavyweight as *The Firm.*[59]

A Controversial Role

After completing *The Firm,* Cruise decided it was time to break new ground. He signed on as the sinister vampire Lestat in *Interview with the Vampire.* This film was based on the enormously popular book by Anne Rice, and there was a great deal of anticipation

Author Anne Rice publicly expressed her outrage that the clean-cut Cruise was cast as the title character in the movie version of Interview with the Vampire.

about the movie version. Cruise would play a villain for the first time. The role required him to lose weight, bleach his hair, take piano lessons, speak with a French accent, and have on-screen love affairs with a man (played by Brad Pitt) and a young girl (played by twelve-year-old Kirsten Dunst).

Cruise faced controversy almost from the minute it was announced that he would be playing Lestat. Author Anne Rice was furious at Cruise's casting. She was unable to imagine how the clean-cut, straight-arrow actor could play the bloodthirsty vampire. And she wasn't shy about expressing her feelings. Rice gave many interviews to newspapers and magazines, in which she ridiculed the choice of Cruise. She referred to Tom Cruise and Brad Pitt as "suited to play Huck Finn and Tom Sawyer, not vampires Lestat and Louis. . . . Tom Cruise is a case of ludicrous casting."[60]

Cruise was determined to ignore the criticism and work as hard as ever on the role of Lestat, but he was hurt and dismayed by Rice's attacks. He told *Interview* magazine,

I've had that happen to me before on other movies, although on a smaller scale. With *Born on the Fourth of July* and with *Rain Man* there was controversy, too. Now people view those choices as successes, but before, they were saying, "Why is he choosing to do these roles?" Or "Why did they cast Tom Cruise?" Obviously, a lot of people felt similarly about my playing Lestat. My name is bigger now;

Cruise's portrayal of the vampire Lestat in Interview with the Vampire *won over author Anne Rice and proved his versatility as an actor.*

I'm a bigger target. This time around, it hit the front pages of newspapers and television. Maybe to other people it looks as if I haven't challenged myself as an actor, but every step of the way, I've pushed myself as hard as I could. So with this role, I remember being so surprised by the controversy and thinking, What the hell is this? I remember being very hurt, actually. But my whole life, there have been those who have told me I can't do this or that. You know, "You're going to fail. Why are you trying to do it?" When I wanted to become an actor, they'd say, "What are you doing with your life?". . . . The thing is that I love acting, pushing myself, and exploring.[61]

After seeing a prerelease copy of the film, Anne Rice changed her mind about Tom Cruise. She took out a full-page ad in *Variety* magazine to apologize for her previous statements about him. She told the media how impressed she was with Cruise's performance and expressed satisfaction with Cruise's casting as Lestat. The film's producer, David Geffen, told *Entertainment Weekly* that "She [Rice] loves it. The movie and the performances were beyond her wildest expectations—and, by the way, she thought Tom was incredible."[62]

Interview with the Vampire went on to commercial success. Once again, Cruise had proved he could play roles beyond that of the clean-cut, handsome, all-American hero. As he explained to *Interview* magazine,

Image . . . is something that's created by the press, by different audiences on particular movies. All actors go up against this. It's frustrating, actually. Incredibly frustrating. But as an actor, you don't allow yourself to get locked into that. I feel for actors, because I know they hear all the time how they can't do it: "Well, you don't look the role." There's not a lot of imagination.[63]

New Challenges

By the mid-1990s, Cruise was ready to move beyond acting. He wanted more control over the movies he starred in. To further this

What Does a Producer Do, Anyway?

The producer is one of the most important people on any movie set. The producer and his or her production company are responsible for turning an idea into a movie. It is the producer's job to come up with the money to make the film by obtaining financing from movie studios or investors; hire the director, actors, and technical staff; supervise the making of the movie; and arrange for the finished film to be distributed to theaters.

Movie studios often provide producers with the money to make movies. The studio sends a representative to the movie set to supervise the production and make sure the studio's money is being spent wisely; this person is often called the executive producer. Other people who contribute money, time, or creative energy are listed as associate producers in a film's credits.

ambition, he formed Cruise/Wagner Productions with his longtime publicist and friend, Paula Wagner. Their first project was producing *Mission: Impossible,* a movie based on a popular TV series from the late 1960s. Along with producing, Cruise would also star as secret agent Ethan Hunt and do most of his own stunts while filming the dangerous action sequences that make up much of the film.

The double roles of producer and star made Cruise "a walking—no, make that running—talking advertisement for the 27-hour day,"[64] according to Tom Friend of *Premiere* magazine. Determined to keep the film within its $64 million budget, Cruise did not take his usual salary, which was now up to $20 million per picture. Instead, he would receive a percentage of the profits. This turned out to be a wise financial move since Cruise's share of the movie's profits turned out to be much more than $20 million.

Cruise was not afraid to clash with the film's director, Brian De Palma. As always, Cruise was determined to be in control, and his hands-on attitude led to some battles. "Yep, no shortage of opinions on this movie," reported one of the film's writers, David Koepp. "No one was going to roll over and let the other's creative opinion rule the day."[65]

Cruise was determined to surround himself with people who supported his vision for the movie and who were just as hardworking and dedicated as he was. "There were a couple of people who said, 'Can't do, can't do, can't do,'" Cruise admitted. Those people didn't last long on the set. But coworkers who shared

Cruise's work ethic were invited to join him for dinner or other social events. One of the movie's costars, Henry Czerny, told *Premiere* magazine, "If he likes your energy and it jells with his, no question he's thrilled with you."[66]

Mission: Impossible went on to become a blockbuster, grossing more than $400 million. Cruise's production company was off to a flying start.

Real-Life Heroics

Cruise performed daring feats not only on-screen but in real life as well. In 1996, he saw a woman get hit by a car in Los Angeles. Cruise

Director Brian De Palma consults with Cruise during the filming of the blockbuster Mission: Impossible.

rushed to her side, phoned for help on his car phone, and stayed with her until paramedics arrived. Then he followed the ambulance to UCLA Medical Center to make sure the woman was all right. When Cruise discovered that she had no health insurance, he paid her entire hospital bill.

A few years later, Cruise hurried to the aid of victims in a boating accident off the island of Capri in Italy, and in London called an ambulance and gave aid to the victim of a car accident. Cruise was quick to help others but wished he had more privacy to respond to people in need. As he put it, "It's not the greatest thing in the world to be rescued by me. The next day, everyone comes knocking on your door."[67]

Walking on the Dark Side

Cruise followed up his success in *Mission: Impossible* with *Jerry Maguire*, in which he played the title character, a sports agent who battles cynicism and jealousy to discover the importance of loyalty, friendship, and love. The part was similar to earlier Cruise roles. Once again, he was playing a likable character who overcomes obstacles to become a better person. Cruise admitted he

> just related to the character emotionally. I meet these people and I wonder what their lives are like. Is this the person I want to be? Are they where they want to be? That's what appealed to me about Maguire. Jerry's one of those guys I've always wondered about.[68]

Jerry Maguire was a huge success, both critically and commercially. The role brought Cruise his second Oscar® nomination. Once again, however, he was passed over for the Best Actor Award, although costar Cuba Gooding Jr. did win for best supporting actor.

Cruise's next two roles were an abrupt departure from the character of Jerry Maguire. As he had done with *Interview with the Vampire,* Cruise decided to turn to the dark side of human nature. Along with his wife, Nicole Kidman, Cruise signed on to star in Stanley Kubrick's *Eyes Wide Shut.*

Kubrick was a legendary director who had made such classic films as *Dr. Strangelove* and *2001: A Space Odyssey.* Cruise jumped at

Cruise and Cuba Gooding Jr. in a scene from Jerry Maguire. *Both actors were nominated for Academy Awards, but only Gooding went home with one.*

the chance to work with him. But making the movie was a demanding experience. The original eighteen-week filming schedule stretched out to fifty-two weeks between November 1996 and June 1998. Cruise and Kidman moved their family—which now included two small children—to London for the making of the film. And Cruise turned down about $60 million in other acting jobs to work with Kubrick.

Eyes Wide Shut was an emotional challenge for the couple as well. Playing a husband and wife who explore the darkest aspects of their relationship put pressure on Cruise and Kidman's own

Stanley Kubrick

During Stanley Kubrick's career as a director, he took on many challenging projects. He often explored the darker side of human nature, taking on such topics as war, violence, mental instability, and sexual tension. He is considered one of the greatest directors of all time.

Kubrick was born in New York City in 1928. His earliest movies were short documentaries. His first feature-length movies, *Fear and Desire* (1953), *Killer's Kiss* (1955), and *The Killing* (1956), were commercial failures but received some good reviews. His next movie, *Paths of Glory* (1957), was set during World War I and received great critical acclaim. Then Kubrick made *Spartacus* (1960), the story of a slave who leads a rebellion in ancient Rome. The film was a huge box office hit and is now considered a classic.

Over the next thirty years, Kubrick became known for his vivid depictions of violence and his use of stunning special effects. He made a number of unforgettable films, including *Lolita* (1962), *Dr. Strangelove, Or How I Learned to Stop Worrying and Love the Bomb* (1964), *2001: A Space Odyssey* (1968), *A Clockwork Orange* (1971), *Barry Lyndon* (1975), *The Shining* (1980), and *Full Metal Jacket* (1987). He was nominated for a best director Oscar® for *Dr. Strangelove, 2001: A Space Odyssey*, and *Barry Lyndon*. *Dr. Strangelove* and *Barry Lyndon* were nominated for best picture. Kubrick had just completed his last movie, *Eyes Wide Shut*, when he died in 1999.

Stanley Kubrick is widely regarded as one of the greatest directors of all time.

marriage, which Cruise has admitted is "not always perfect." Actor Todd Field, who also worked on the film, recalled that their scenes together "were really profound and uncomfortable. The notes they were hitting were notes you can't act; there was real stuff there."[69]

Then, in March 1999, just three months before *Eyes Wide Shut* premiered, Kubrick died suddenly of a heart attack. Cruise was devastated. The two men had become very close over the course of working on the movie. Kubrick's longtime assistant, Leon Vitali, described their friendship as "the most established relationship I've seen in 30 years between Stanley and one of his stars. And the deeper they got into filming, the more relaxed and open it became." Kubrick's close friend, Julian Senior, agreed, saying that Kubrick became "a surrogate father figure" to Cruise. "They spent a lot of mornings together, and Stanley spent a lot of time with their kids."[70] Cruise received word of Kubrick's death in a phone call from Vitali in the middle of the night. He later recalled hearing the news as "that moment of real loss and pain that I hadn't felt in a while. I mean shock—absolute shock. . . . That was a very difficult time."[71]

Eyes Wide Shut was a huge disappointment both critically and commercially. The film made $55 million, far less than most Cruise

Cruise and Kidman in a scene from Eyes Wide Shut. *Highly anticipated, the movie turned out to be a huge critical and commercial disappointment.*

films. Audiences hated the film's dark, confusing story. According to Cinemascore president Edward Mintz, whose company tracks opening-night responses, the film received some of the worst grades he'd ever seen: "73 percent of people 25 and over gave it an F. You start getting Ds and Fs, a movie shouldn't have even been made."[72]

Cruise's portrayal of arrogant infomercial pitchman Frank Mackey in Magnolia *earned him a Golden Globe Award and an Academy Award nomination for best supporting actor.*

Cruise was disappointed by the critical and commercial response to *Eyes Wide Shut*. But he was already involved with another challenging role. In the film *Magnolia*, Cruise played Frank Mackey, an arrogant, nasty infomercial pitchman who hides deep secrets from his past. Cruise relished the challenges of the role. "With *Magnolia* I thought, This, this could be wild. I mean, I could *really* fail here. . . . This could be a real pie in the face . . . I've gotta do it!"[73]

One of the film's most wrenching scenes was a deathbed reconciliation between Cruise's character and his dying father, who was played by Jason Robards. Cruise tried to downplay the scene's connection to his own troubled relationship with his father, saying, "You know, it's a character but it does have elements. . . . I'll tell you, I was nervous letting my mother see this . . . the emotional aspect of it."[74] Cruise was worried about how his mother would react to the intense emotions on the screen and feared she would be upset by the memories the movie would stir up from their own family experiences. To protect his mother's privacy, he arranged for her to view the movie at a private screening, rather than have to watch the film with a large audience.

Cruise won critical acclaim for his role in *Magnolia* and was nominated for a Golden Globe and an Oscar® for best supporting actor. As with *Born on the Fourth of July*, Cruise won the Golden Globe, but not the Oscar®. He brushed off his disappointment at never winning an Oscar®, saying, "I never let myself expect too much with things . . . [except for] my work."[75]

Back to the Future

As always, work was at the front of Cruise's mind, and he was already involved with another movie project. Cruise's production company, Cruise/Wagner Productions, was back in action in the summer of 2000 with the release of the *Mission: Impossible* sequel, *M:I-2*. As in the first *Mission: Impossible* film, Cruise did many of his own stunts. One of the most dangerous had Cruise dangling from a cliff—a scene that had executive producer Terence Chang looking away in fear. "He can jump up and kick someone in the face and then flip backwards. You'd be amazed!"[76] Chang enthused about Cruise's physical abilities. Cruise's eagerness to do his own stunts may have made his professional colleagues—and his wife—nervous. But it did not stop him

Cruise scales a steep cliff in the Mission: Impossible *sequel, M:I-2. In both films Cruise insisted on performing most of his own stunts.*

from taking risks and accepting challenges—something he had always loved to do.

What does the future hold for Tom Cruise? It's safe to say he will continue to play blockbuster parts. He will continue to take chances and stretch his abilities as an actor. And he intends to stay on top. He told *Talk* magazine

I don't feel I've done everything that I [want to] do. Look, I feel good about stuff I've done and I've learned—good and bad—but I don't feel like I've *done* it yet. I don't feel like I'm . . . finished. In acting, as good as you are today, it's a different experience every time you go out, every movie. . . . There's no rulebook as to what a great movie is, or what a perfect moment is. It changes, and you have to keep evolving. You've got to keep working—and that's what's fun. That's the challenge of it.[77]

Cruise has always looked for new challenges in his professional life. But he tried to keep his personal life relaxed, steady, and focused. His devotion to his wife and children shows another side of his personality.

Chapter 5

Family Life

TOM CRUISE IS devoted to his career, but he is even more devoted to his family. His marriage to Nicole Kidman is considered one of the strongest unions in Hollywood, and he is a hands-on father to the couple's two children, Isabella and Connor.

One of the strongest bonds between Cruise and Kidman seems to be their mutual respect for each other. Kidman is not a behind-the-scenes wife who is seldom seen in public. On the contrary, she has her own thriving acting career and does not share all of her husband's interests. Because of the example set by his mother, Cruise has always admired strong women. "I like someone who's independent," Cruise confided to *Redbook* magazine. "The thing about Nic is that she has her own career. It challenges me."[78]

Kidman also thinks the close relationship between Cruise and his mother and sisters has affected how he feels about his wife and about women in general. "Tom and his sisters went through so much together," she once said. "You can feel their bond. I hope Tom, [son] Connor, [daughter] Bella and I have the same intensity of love."[79]

Although many celebrity couples live separate lives, Cruise has made it clear that his relationship with Kidman is the most important thing in his life. He refuses to let their professional commitments get in the way of spending time together. He told *Vanity Fair* magazine, "I go where she's going. Or she goes where I go. We're always working and on the road, so Nic is my best friend."[80] When Kidman was appearing in the play *The Blue Room* in London, Cruise and their children moved there so that the family would not be separated. And when Cruise is away from home filming movies, Kidman and the children go with him.

Cruise once told *Redbook* that Kidman was "my best friend, my lover, the mother of my children, my wife, and my confidant. When I read *Jerry Maguire*, I was crying, because that line 'You complete me' is how I feel about her."[81] Indeed, the couple and their children have such a tight family unit that few other people

Kidman and Cruise take a walk through Central Park with Isabella, their daughter. A devoted husband and father, Cruise refuses to let the demands of his career keep him from spending time with his family.

Cruise and Kidman appear to have a close relationship that has so far overcome the difficulties that many celebrity couples face.

are part of their social circle. Rather than attend Hollywood parties, the couple might go out to dinner together, then come home and spend time with their children.

The Press Attacks

Although Cruise and Kidman have a strong bond, their relationship has been the target of many false rumors and gossip. There is a long-standing story that the marriage is simply a business arrangement to cover the fact that Cruise is homosexual. According to this rumor, Kidman married Cruise in order to win better acting roles for herself. Cruise and Kidman have long denied this rumor. Cruise complained to *Talk* magazine,

> They're saying you're a liar. Everything that is so sacred, that I feel so personally and deeply. . . . Basically, people are saying, "That's a lie, it's a sham." At a certain point I said, "Fine, go ahead and prove it. Go ahead. You've said these things about me? Now I want an apology. . . . Prove that we're liars." [82]

Kidman has also complained about the story: "I've spent a lot of time building up a career and my first love is acting. . . . I'm not blowing my own trumpet here, but it makes me irritated because you never get the part unless you come up with the goods. Studios have millions of dollars riding on these movies and they're not going to go,

Those Annoying Tabloids

Tabloids are newspapers and magazines which report rumors about celebrities that may or may not be true. These papers have a reputation for exaggerating the truth and even making up stories altogether. For example, if a celebrity is slightly ill, a tabloid may report that he or she is at death's door. Many celebrities have sued tabloids for printing false information and won. The tabloids usually have to pay money to the celebrity, which he or she often donates to charity, and issue a statement saying the original story was false.

Tabloids are also known for publishing intrusive photographs. Tabloid photographers or paparazzi have been known to climb walls to photograph celebrities and their families in the privacy of their homes or backyards. They also confront them in public and even provoke confrontations in order to get a good photograph and an exciting story. Several celebrities have been arrested for assaulting tabloid photographers who tried to take pictures when the celebrity and his or her family did not want to be bothered. Many stars are especially sensitive to having their children photographed or harassed in public.

Despite their often unethical ways of getting stories, tabloids have sometimes managed to report truthful stories before the mainstream media. And tabloids have a huge audience of people who simply cannot get enough news about their favorite stars—whether that news is true or not!

'Let's please Tom and put Nicole in this movie.' It just doesn't work that way."[83]

Cruise and Kidman have gone as far as suing magazines that printed untrue stories about them. In 1998, they sued the British tabloid *The Express* for publishing a story about Cruise's supposed homosexuality and the couple's false marriage. They won $330,000

Cruise speaks to the press after winning a libel suit against a British tabloid.

and donated the money to charity. Cruise did not file the lawsuit to protect his own image; he did it because he was afraid his children would hear the rumors and be hurt by them. Cruise explained, "They . . . said some brutal things about my children. I just go, 'You know what, guys? This is not okay. My kids go to school, and they have friends, and things go out on the Internet. Stop it. It is not okay.'"[84] Cruise is fiercely determined to protect his children and make their growing-up years as normal and happy as possible.

Other stories have reported that Cruise and Kidman are constantly fighting. Cruise jokingly admits that the two do fight, "usually about who is more tired."[85] But he also says, "There are moments when we say this honeymoon is on pause for the next two hours while we get things worked out. You really only learn about yourself by that stuff that bounces back in your face."[86] All in all, Cruise and Kidman seem to have an enormously close, loving relationship.

A Growing Family

From the early days of their marriage, Cruise and Kidman were eager to expand their family. They chose to do so through adoption. In 1993, the couple adopted a baby girl and named her Isabella Jane Kidman Cruise. Two years later, the couple added a newborn son, Connor Antony Kidman Cruise.

Because his own father was absent during much of his childhood, Cruise is determined to be an involved father to his children. He and Kidman take the children with them when they are filming movies. "Tom is the greatest dad, and he finds time to be that guy," said Cameron Crowe, the director of *Jerry Maguire*. "I see how attentive he is to his kids without a huge deal being made."[87]

Cruise's costars on *Mission: Impossible* soon became used to the presence of baby Connor on the set. When the cameras were running, Cruise was all business. But as soon as the actors took a break, his focus shifted right back to his family. Costar Jon Voight told *McCall's* that "We'd finish a scene, and he'd nearly run from the set to his camper to check on his kids. Connor was just an infant, and Tom was always walking around with the baby strapped to him."[88]

Although much of their time is spent on movie sets, Cruise and Kidman are also determined to give their children a normal life. "All the kids in L.A. get Ferraris when they're 16," Cruise told an Australian magazine in 1996, "and there's just no way . . . that's ever going to happen with ours."[89] And he told *People,* "We read to our children every night before they go to bed. We work our schedules around them."[90] Cruise and Kidman face different challenges than most couples when it comes to combining their careers and their families. By placing the emphasis on spending time with their children, the couple do their best to ensure that the children have a stable, loving home—even if that home happens to be a movie set in a foreign city.

Cruise confesses that the couple's schedules do lead to some unusual interactions with the children. He told *People,*

> Sometimes we go out to dinner and stay up until about 2, 3 in the morning and wake up the kids. They chat and play games, and they go back to sleep. It's wild. What is right? What is wrong? As long as we're together, that is the most important thing.[91]

The fact that Isabella and Connor are adopted has led to even more speculation and gossip from the press. The couple has said that their decision to adopt is a private matter, and they refuse to discuss whether they are physically unable to have children. "We adopted Isabella because she was meant for us,"[92] Nicole Kidman has said. Like Cruise, she didn't feel the need to explain their choices or discuss the matter in any more detail.

In fact, when a reporter for *Premiere* magazine said, "Imagine if they were [Cruise's] own children," the actor became quite angry. "These are my own," he responded. "These *are* my own two kids. . . . Look, we wanted to adopt. But *these* children, they couldn't be *my* children any more. . . . These are my kids. Without question."[93]

Another subject of press interest is the fact that Connor is African American. But once again, Cruise has said that his children's background is a private matter:

> That's his story, and our story together, and I don't want our relationship—and the same goes for Isabella—to be defined before he can define it himself. And if he

wants to tell his story when he grows up, you know, he'll tell his story.[94]

Meanwhile, Cruise, Kidman, and the children just want to be left alone to live their lives in private.

Kidman and Cruise (pictured with their children Isabella and Connor) refuse to discuss with the press their decision to adopt and the background of their children.

Religious Beliefs

Another area of Cruise's life that he feels is a private matter is his religion. Cruise is a member of the controversial Church of Scientology. He was introduced to Scientology by his first wife, Mimi Rogers, sometime before 1989. Rogers' father was a founding member of the church.

The Church of Scientology

The Church of Scientology was founded by science-fiction writer L. Ron Hubbard during the 1950s. Hubbard is best known for his *Battlefield Earth* series of novels. He created a process called *dianetics*, a method of spiritual healing that aims to improve a person's mental health by helping him or her confront painful memories. In 1950, Hubbard wrote a book called *Dianetics: The Modern Science of Mental Health*, which became a best-seller.

The Church of Scientology presently has 8 million members around the world and centers in more than seventy countries. The church has said its goal is to help people understand their spiritual side and achieve spiritual balance. To do this, Scientology encourages its members to rid themselves of the painful experiences of their past. This will help them gain confidence and control over themselves and their environment.

Despite widespread criticism of Scientology, the church has many famous members who speak highly of the church and its teachings. John Travolta, Kelly Preston, Kirstie Alley, Jenna Elfman, Priscilla Presley, and Lisa Marie Presley are just a few of the celebrities who belong to the church.

John Travolta signs copies of the bestseller Battlefield Earth *to promote his appearance in the movie version of the book by Church of Scientology founder L. Ron Hubbard.*

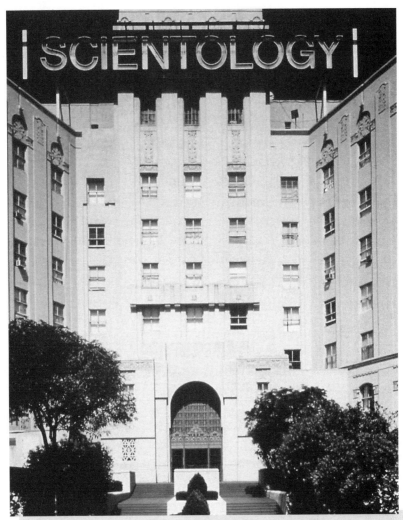

Although some critics of the Church of Scientology liken it to a cult, Cruise has only positive things to say about his membership in the church.

The Church of Scientology has many critics, some of whom call the church a cult. They say Scientology tries to take control of every part of its members' lives. Members are encouraged to cut off relationships with people who do not support Scientology's teachings and goals. The religion also has many rules to dictate what its members can and cannot do, and it has been accused of brainwashing individuals so that they can no longer think for themselves. People who have left the church accuse other Scientologists of threatening them, both professionally and personally, in order to prevent them from breaking free of the religion. But loyal members of Scientology say these accusations are not true and that the church helps people refocus their lives and have a more positive mental outlook. Many people assert they have been helped by the church's teachings and practices.

Cruise himself has nothing but good things to say about the church. He has credited Scientology with helping him overcome his dyslexia. He also says that Scientology has helped him become a better person and actor. "Essentially, it's enabled me—it's just helped me to become more me. It gives me certain tools to utilize to be the person I want to be and explore the areas I want to explore as an artist."[95] In any case, Cruise has said that his religion is a personal matter, and he refuses to discuss his beliefs or his membership in the church with the press.

Hard Work Pays Off

Throughout his career, Tom Cruise has displayed incredible drive, focus, and determination. He's not afraid to work hard and throw himself completely into a role. Cruise brings that same dedication to his personal life. He understands that success is not only measured in box office dollars alone, but in having a family to love and cherish. In both his professional and personal lives, Tom Cruise has worked hard to become a success.

Notes

Chapter 1: Growing Up—and Taking Chare

1. Quoted in Wensley Clarkson, *Tom Cruise: Unauthorized*. Norwalk, CT: Hastings House, 1997, p. 10.
2. Quoted in Tom Friend, "Man with a Mission," *Premiere*, June 1996, p. 70.
3. Quoted in Clarkson, *Tom Cruise: Unauthorized*, p. 12.
4. Quoted in Clarkson, *Tom Cruise: Unauthorized*, p. 59.
5. Quoted in Clarkson, *Tom Cruise: Unauthorized*, p. 25.
6. Quoted in Chris Connelly, "How Tom Cruise Keeps His Edge," *Talk*, April 2000, p. 125.
7. Quoted in Jill Smolowe, "The Baby Boom's Biggest Star Stayed Grounded, Despite a Broken Home, Dyslexia—and a Pesky Press," *People Weekly*, March 15, 1999, p. 130.
8. Quoted in Friend, "Man with a Mission," p. 70.
9. Quoted in Friend, "Man with a Mission," p. 70.
10. Quoted in Clarkson, *Tom Cruise: Unauthorized*, p. 21.
11. Quoted in Connelly, "How Tom Cruise Keeps His Edge," p. 177.
12. Quoted in Smolowe, "The Baby Boom's Biggest Star," p. 130.
13. Quoted in Alex Tresniowski, "Man of Action," *People Weekly*, May 22, 2000, p. 141.
14. Quoted in Clarkson, *Tom Cruise: Unauthorized*, p. 46.

Chapter 2: Early Struggles and Successes

15. Quoted in Clarkson, *Tom Cruise: Unauthorized*, p. 65.
16. Quoted in Clarkson, *Tom Cruise: Unauthorized*, p. 65.
17. Quoted in Clarkson, *Tom Cruise: Unauthorized*, p. 80.
18. Quoted in Clarkson, *Tom Cruise: Unauthorized*, p. 80.

19. Quoted in Phal Vaughter, "The People Profiles: Tom Cruise." PEOPLE.com.,www.people.aol.com/people/pprofiles/biography/biography/0,3375,96,00.html.

20. Quoted in Clarkson, *Tom Cruise: Unauthorized*, p. 84.

21. Quoted in Clarkson, *Tom Cruise: Unauthorized*, p. 89.

22. Quoted in Clarkson, *Tom Cruise: Unauthorized*, p. 94.

23. Quoted in Clarkson, *Tom Cruise: Unauthorized*, p. 102.

24. Quoted in Clarkson, *Tom Cruise: Unauthorized*, p. 109.

25. Quoted in David Hutchings, "No Wonder Tom Cruise Is Sitting Pretty—*Risky Business* Has Paid Off in Stardom," *People Weekly*, September 5, 1983, p. 107.

26. Quoted in Hutchings, "No Wonder Tom Cruise Is Sitting Pretty," p. 107.

27. Quoted in Hutchings, "No Wonder Tom Cruise Is Sitting Pretty," p. 107.

28. Quoted in Clarkson, *Tom Cruise: Unauthorized*, p. 155.

29. Quoted in Clarkson, *Tom Cruise: Unauthorized*, p. 161.

30. Clarkson, *Tom Cruise: Unauthorized*, p. 163.

31. Quoted in Clarkson, *Tom Cruise: Unauthorized*, p. 173.

32. Quoted in Clarkson, *Tom Cruise: Unauthorized*, p. 182.

33. Quoted in Connelly, "How Tom Cruise Keeps His Edge," p. 178.

34. Vaughter, "The People Profiles: Tom Cruise."

35. Quoted in Vaughter, "The People Profiles: Tom Cruise."

Chapter 3: Working with Giants

36. Quoted in Clarkson, *Tom Cruise: Unauthorized*, p. 203.

37. Quoted in Smolowe, "The Baby Boom's Biggest Star," p. 130.

38. Quoted in Clarkson, *Tom Cruise: Unauthorized*, p. 202.

39. Quoted in Clarkson, *Tom Cruise: Unauthorized*, p. 210.

40. Quoted in Clarkson, *Tom Cruise: Unauthorized*, p. 209.

41. Quoted in Clarkson, *Tom Cruise: Unauthorized*, p. 224.

42. Quoted in Connelly, "How Tom Cruise Keeps His Edge," p. 176.

43. Quoted in Clarkson, *Tom Cruise: Unauthorized*, p. 235.

44. Quoted in Jennet Conant, "The Professional," *Vanity Fair*, June 1996, p. 183.

45. Quoted in Clarkson, *Tom Cruise: Unauthorized*, p. 238.

46. Quoted in Clarkson, *Tom Cruise: Unauthorized,* p. 240.
47. Quoted in Clarkson, *Tom Cruise: Unauthorized,* p. 241.
48. Quoted in Connelly, "How Tom Cruise Keeps His Edge," p. 176.
49. Quoted in Clarkson, *Tom Cruise: Unauthorized,* p. 261.
50. Quoted in Clarkson, *Tom Cruise: Unauthorized,* p. 262.
51. Quoted in Clarkson, *Tom Cruise: Unauthorized,* p. 266.
52. Quoted in Clarkson, *Tom Cruise: Unauthorized,* p. 269.
53. Quoted in Friend, "Man with a Mission," p. 72.
54. Quoted in Conant, "The Professional," p. 183.

Chapter 4: Taking Control

55. Quoted in Clarkson, *Tom Cruise: Unauthorized,* p. 322.
56. Quoted in Conant, "The Professional," p. 183.
57. Quoted in Rosemarie Lennon, "Tom Terrific," *McCall's,* July 2000, p. 22.
58. Quoted in Clarkson, *Tom Cruise: Unauthorized,* p. 378.
59. Clarkson, *Tom Cruise: Unauthorized,* p. 379.
60. Quoted in Mark Dawidziak, "Tom Cruise as Movie Vampire Lestat Is the Cross Anne Rice Has to Bear," *Knight-Ridder/ Tribune News Service,* December 3, 1993.
61. Quoted in Ingrid Sischy, "The Interview, the Vampire, the Actor," *Interview,* November 1994, p. 100.
62. Quoted in Richard Natale, "Rice Caves," *Entertainment Weekly,* September 30, 1994, p. 9.
63. Quoted in Sischy, "The Interview," p. 100.
64. Friend, "Man with a Mission," p. 71.
65. Quoted in Friend, "Man with a Mission," p. 72.
66. Quoted in Friend, "Man with a Mission," p. 72.
67. Quoted in Smolowe, "The Baby Boom's Biggest Star," p. 130.
68. Quoted in Clarkson, *Tom Cruise: Unauthorized,* p. 452.
69. Quoted in Tresniowski, "Man of Action," p. 141.
70. Quoted in Tresniowski, "Man of Action," p. 141.
71. Quoted in Connelly, "How Tom Cruise Keeps His Edge," p. 177.
72. Quoted in Tom Gliatto, "Even as Tom and Nicole's Latest Film Suffers at the Box Office, They Take Comfort in Each Other," *People Weekly,* August 16, 1999, p. 68.
73. Quoted in Connelly, "How Tom Cruise Keeps His Edge," p. 125.
74. Quoted in Connelly, "How Tom Cruise Keeps His Edge," p. 176.

75. Quoted in Connelly, "How Tom Cruise Keeps His Edge," p. 125.
76. Quoted in Tresniowski, "Man of Action," p. 141.
77. Quoted in Connelly, "How Tom Cruise Keeps His Edge," p. 125.

Chapter 5: Family Life

78. Quoted in Debra Birbaum, "What My Family Taught Me About Love," *Redbook,* November 1999, p. 69.
79. Quoted in Lennon, "Tom Terrific," p. 26.
80. Quoted in Conant, "The Professional," p. 184.
81. Quoted in Birbaum, "What My Family Taught Me About Love," p. 69.
82. Quoted in Connelly, "How Tom Cruise Keeps His Edge," p. 177.
83. Quoted in Clarkson, *Tom Cruise: Unauthorized,* pp. 303–304.
84. Quoted in Smolowe, "The Baby Boom's Biggest Star," p. 130.
85. Quoted in Lennon, "Tom Terrific," p. 26.
86. Quoted in Smolowe, "The Baby Boom's Biggest Star," p. 130.
87. Quoted in Tresniowski, "Man of Action," p. 138.
88. Quoted in Lennon, "Tom Terrific," p. 20.
89. Quoted in Gliatto, "Even as Tom and Nicole's Latest Film Suffers at the Box Office, They Take Comfort in Each Other," p. 78.
90. Quoted in Smolowe, "The Baby Boom's Biggest Star," p. 130.
91. Quoted in Smolowe, "The Baby Boom's Biggest Star," p. 130.
92. Quoted in Friend, "Man with a Mission," p. 74.
93. Quoted in Friend, "Man with a Mission," p. 74.
94. Quoted in Friend, "Man with a Mission," p. 103.
95. Quoted in Clarkson, *Tom Cruise: Unauthorized,* p. 347.

Important Dates in the Life of Tom Cruise

1962

Thomas Cruise Mapother IV is born in Syracuse, New York.

1974

Cruise's parents divorce.

1978

Cruise's mother, Mary Lee Pfeiffer, marries Jack South.

1980

Cruise stars in his high school's production of *Guys and Dolls* and decides to become an actor. He moves to New York City in June to pursue his career.

1981

Appears in his first movie, *Endless Love.*

1983

Has his first starring role and biggest commercial success so far in *Risky Business.*

1986

Stars in *Top Gun,* which vaults him to superstardom.

1987

Marries Mimi Rogers.

1990

Receives his first Oscar® nomination for *Born on the Fourth of July.* Divorces Mimi Rogers and marries Nicole Kidman.

1993
Adopts Isabella Jane Kidman Cruise.

1995
Adopts Connor Antony Kidman Cruise.

1996
Produces and stars in *Mission: Impossible,* one of the biggest money-making films in history.

1997
Nominated for his second Oscar® for *Jerry Maguire.*

2000
Nominated for his third Oscar® for *Magnolia.*

For Further Reading

Books

Julie S. Bach, *Tom Cruise: Movie Star.* Edina, MN: Abdo and Daughters, 1993. A brief, easy-to-read overview of Cruise's career and personal life.

Deborah Kent, *Extraordinary People with Disabilities.* New York: Children's Press, 1996. Includes an entry on Cruise, focusing on how he overcame his learning disability.

Phelan Powell, *Tom Cruise.* Philadelphia, PA: Chelsea House Publishers, 1999. An in-depth look at Cruise's personal and professional lives.

Periodicals

Rosemarie Lennon, "Tom Terrific," *McCall's,* July 2000.

Jill Smolowe, "The Baby Boom's Biggest Star Stayed Grounded, Despite a Broken Home, Dyslexia—and a Pesky Press," *People Weekly,* March 15, 1999.

Internet Sources

Celebsites (www.celebsites.com). Type in Cruise's name for a comprehensive list of Web sites devoted to him.

PEOPLE.com (www.people.aol.com). Click on "People Profiles," then type in Cruise's name. You can also access past *People Weekly* magazine articles about the star from this Web site.

Works Consulted

Books

Clarkson, Wensley, *Tom Cruise: Unauthorized.* Norwalk, CT: Hastings House, 1997. An in-depth look at Cruise's career and personal life.

Periodicals

Debra Birbaum, "What My Family Taught Me About Love," *Redbook*, November 1999.

Jennet Conant, "Lestat, C'est Moi," *Esquire*, March 1994.

———, "The Professional," *Vanity Fair*, June 1996.

Chris Connelly, "How Tom Cruise Keeps His Edge," *Talk*, April 2000.

Mark Dawidziak, "Tom Cruise as Movie Vampire Lestat Is the Cross Anne Rice Has to Bear," *Knight-Ridder/Tribune News Service*, December 3, 1993.

Tom Friend, "Man With a Mission," *Premiere*, June 1996.

Tom Gliatto, "Even as Tom and Nicole's Latest Film Suffers at the Box Office, They Take Comfort in Each Other," *People Weekly*, August 16, 1999.

David Hutchings, "No Wonder Tom Cruise is Sitting Pretty—*Risky Business* Has Paid Off in Stardom," *People Weekly*, September 5, 1983.

Richard Natale, "Rice Caves," *Entertainment Weekly*, September 30, 1994.

Ingrid Sischy, "The Interview, the Vampire, the Actor," *Interview*, November 1994.

Alex Tresniowski, "Man of Action," *People Weekly*, May 22, 2000.

Index

Academy Awards, 49, 51
Academy of Motion Picture Arts
  and Sciences, 42
Actors Studio, 42
All the Right Moves (film), 35–36
Alley, Kirstie, 80
American Academy of Dramatic
  Arts, 22
Apocalypse Now (film), 30
autism, 47
auto racing, 53–54

Babbitt, Charlie, 46, 49
Babbitt, Raymond, 46–47, 49
Bacon, Kevin, 58
Barry Lyndon (film), 66
Battlefield Earth (novel series), 80
Becker, Harold, 26
Black Stallion, The (film), 30
Blue Room, The (play), 55, 72
Bonnie and Clyde (film), 53
Born on the Fourth of July (film),
  10, 50–51, 60
Broadway, 22
Bruckheimer, Jerry, 36–38,
  53–54
Butch Cassidy and the Sundance Kid
  (film), 42

car accidents, 63–64
Chang, Terence, 69
Chapman, Michael, 35
Chinatown (film), 53
Church of Scientology. *See*

Scientology
Clarkson, Wensley, 36, 58
Clockwork Orange, A (film), 66
Cocktail (film), 40, 45–46
Color of Money, The (film), 41–43
computer-generated images, 34
Connelly, Chris, 18, 24, 39, 45
Cool Hand Luke (film), 42
Coppola, Francis Ford, 30–31
Corman, Roger, 30
Crowe, Cameron, 77
Cruise, Connor Anthony
  Kidman (son), 72, 77–78
Cruise, Isabella Jane Kidman
  (daughter), 72, 77–78
Cruise, Tom
  attacked by press, 74–77
  becomes interested in acting,
    21, 23
  birth of, 10
  changes name, 15
  childhood of, 10–13
  directs "The Frightening
    Frammies," 58
  education of, 13–14, 18–21
  family life of, 72–74, 77–79
  as film producer, 62
  Golden Globe Awards won by,
    51, 69
  helping accident victims
    63–64
  marriages of
    to Kidman, 55–56
    to Rogers, 44–45

mother's influence on, 18
Oscar nominations of, 51–52,
  64
problems with dyslexia, 9, 14,
  19, 21, 57, 82
protective of mother and sisters,
  17
relationship with reporters,
  32–33
religious beliefs of, 80–82
as teenager, 17
see also names of individual films
Cruise/Wagner Productions, 62,
  69
Czerny, Henry, 63

daydreams, 13
Days of Thunder (film), 40, 53–55
Dead Calm (film), 54–55
Dean, James, 40
December 13 (film), 30
De Mornay, Rebecca (Tom's
  girlfriend), 32
De Palma, Brian, 62
Detroit, Nathan, 21
Dianetics: The Modern Science of
  Mental Health (Hubbard), 80
divorce, 15, 17
Djorjevic, Stefan, 35–36
Dr. Strangelove (film), 64, 66
Dunst, Kirsten, 59
dyslexia, 9, 14, 19, 21, 57, 82

Ebert, Roger, 32
Elfman, Jenna, 80
Endless Love (film), 24
Entertainment Weekly (magazine),
  61
Estevez, Emilio, 26
Express, The (tabloid), 76
Eyes Wide Shut (film), 64–69

Fallen Angels (television series), 58
Fallen Naval Air Station, 38
Far and Away (film), 57
Fear and Desire (film), 66
Felson, Fast Eddie, 42–43
Few Good Men, A (film), 57

Field, Todd, 66
Finn, Huck, 59
Firm, The (film), 57
food stamps, 17
Friend, Tom, 12, 62
Full Metal Jacket (film), 66

Geffen, David, 61
General Electric, 12–13
G-forces, 38
Glen Ridge High School, 21
Godfather, The (film series), 30, 53
Golden Globe Awards, 51, 69
Gooding, Cuba, Jr., 64
Goodsen, Joel, 31–32
Graduate, The (film), 32
Gross, Edward, 49
Guys and Dolls (musical), 21

Hackman, Gene, 43
Hinton, S. E., 30
Hoffman, Dustin, 32, 46–49
Hollywood Foreign Press
  Association, 51
Hornberg, William, 58
Hubbard, L. Ron, 80
Hud (film), 42
Hustler, The (film), 42
Hutchings, David, 32
Hutton, Timothy, 27–28

Interview (magazine), 59, 61
Interview with the Vampire (film),
  58–61

Jack o' the Green, 36
Jerry Maguire (film), 10, 64, 73
Jones, Jennifer, 51
Julliard School of Music, 22

Kidman, Nicole (wife)
  attacked by press, 74–77
  family life of, 72–74, 77–79
  marriage to Tom, 8, 10, 55–56
  see also names of individual films
Killer's Kiss (film), 66
Killing, The (film), 66
Koepp, David, 62

Kovic, Ron, 50–51
Kubrick, Stanley, 64, 66–67

Laserhead, 54
Lauria, Vincent, 42–43
Legend (film), 36
Lestat, 58–60
Levinson, Barry, 47, 49
Lewicki, Claire, 54
Lolita (film), 66
Los Angeles, 22
Losin' It (film), 29
Lukas, Paul, 51

Mackey, Frank, 69
Magnolia (film), 10, 69
Mapother, Lee Anne (sister), 11
Mapother, Marian (sister), 11
Mapother, Thomas Cruise III
  (father), 10, 12–15
Mapother, Thomas Cruise IV.
  See Cruise, Tom
McCall's (magazine), 77
Midway (film), 18
Mintz, Edward, 67
Miramar Naval Air Station, 38
Mission: Impossible (film), 10,
  62–63, 77
M:I-2 (film), 69
Mitchell, Pete "Maverick," 37
Mr. and Mrs. Bridge (film), 42

Neill, Sam, 55
New York City, 22
Newman, Paul, 42–43, 53

"Old Time Rock 'n' Roll" (song),
  32
Oscars
  awarded to
    Paul Newman, 42–43
    Rain Man, 49
  Cruise nominated for, 51–52,
    64
Outsiders, The (film), 30

paparazzi, 32, 75
Paramount, 39

Paths of Glory (film), 66
Patton (film), 30
Penn, Sean, 26, 28
People (magazine), 17–18, 32, 39,
  43, 78
Pfeiffer, Mary Lee (Tom's
  mother), 11–12, 14, 21
photographers, tabloid, 32
Pitt, Brad, 59
Pollack, Sydney, 58
pool, 42–43
Premiere (magazine), 12, 17, 62,
  78
Presley, Lisa Marie, 80
Presley, Priscilla, 80
Preston, Kelly, 80

Rachel, Rachel (film), 42
Rain Man (film), 10, 46–49, 60
Randle, Steve, 30
Redbook (magazine), 72–73
Redford, Robert, 42
reporters, tabloid, 32–33
Rice, Anne, 58–59, 61
Risky Business (film), 31–32, 52
Robards, Jason, 69
Rogers, Mimi (wife), 44–45, 80
Rumble Fish (film), 30

Sawyer, Tom, 59
Scientology, 80–82
Scorsese, Martin, 42–43
Scott, Tony, 37–38, 54
Secret Garden, The (film), 30
Senior, Julian, 67
Shawn, David, 26, 29
Shining, The (film), 66
Showtime, 58
Simpson, Don, 36–38, 53–54
Song of Bernadette, The (film), 51
South, Jack (stepfather), 20–21
Spartacus (film), 66
Star Wars (film), 18
St. Francis Seminary, 18–19
Sting, The (film), 42
Stone, Oliver, 50, 52
St. Xavier High School, 20
stunts, 34

Summer Wishes, Winter Dreams (film), 42
Sweet Bird of Youth (film), 42

tabloids, 32, 75
Talk (magazine), 18, 39, 45, 70, 75
Taps (film), 26–29, 52
"The Frightening Frammies" (television episode), 58
Three Faces of Eve, The (film), 42
To Die For (film), 55
Top Gun (film), 36–40, 52–53
Towne, Robert, 53–54
Travolta, John, 80

2001: A Space Odyssey (film), 64, 66
UCLA Medical Center, 64

Vanity Fair (magazine), 56, 72
Variety (magazine), 61
Vitali, Leon, 67
Voight, Jon, 77

Wagner, Paula, 62
Watch on the Rhine, The (film), 51
Woodward, Joanne, 42
World War II, 51

Yale School of Drama, 42

Picture Credits

Cover: Frank Edwards/Fotos International/Archive Photos
AFP/Corbis: 76,80
AP World Wide Photos: 8,48,74,79
Archive Photo: 56
Bettman/Corbis:52
Corbis:44,46
Fotos International/Archive Photo:81
Joan Slatkin/Archive Photo:22
Mitchell Gerber/Corbis:73
Photofest: 19, 20, 27, 28, 31, 33, 35, 37-39, 41, 47, 50, 53, 55,
     57, 59,60,63, 65-68,70
Reuters Newmedia/Corbis: 51
Steve Granitz/Retna Ltd.:16
Universal Pictures/Archive Photo:25
Walter McBride/Retna Ltd.: 11
Will and Deni McIntyre/Photo Researchers:15

About the Author

Joanne Mattern is the author of more than one hundred nonfiction and fiction books for children. Her favorite subjects are animals and nature, but she has also written biographies of explorers and sports figures, an encyclopedia on American immigration, classic novel retellings, and activity books. Ms. Mattern lives in New York state with her husband and young daughter.